810.9 R727i
Irish-American
autobiography :the divided
hearts of athletes, priests
Rogers, James

Irish-American Autobiography

Irish-American Autobiography

The Divided Hearts of Athletes, Priests, Pilgrims, and More

James Silas Rogers

The Catholic University of America Press
Washington, D.C.

The paper used in this publication meets the minimum
requirements of American National Standards for Information
Science—Permanence of Paper for Printed Library Materials,
ANSI Z39.48-1984.
∞

Cataloging-in-Publication Data available from the Library
of Congress
ISBN 978-0-8132-2918-8

for Charlie Fanning

Contents

Introduction

⟳

The "Ethnic Fade" That Never Quite Happened

I admit that—however modest its contributions to the study of Irish-American writing may prove in the end—I do look on this book with a bit of a valedictory spirit. Because its subject is, after all, Irish-American autobiography, I will indulge in a small bit of autobiography by way of introduction.

This project has been a long time a-brewing. In 1976, in the opening flourish of the "roots" phenomenon, I hit on the idea of doing Irish Studies as a self-designed undergraduate major (mostly because I was taking incompletes in all the other classes). Four years later, things took another turn when I went to my first meeting of the ACIS, the American Conference for Irish Studies, hosted by the great historian Emmet Larkin at the University of Chicago. In the company of those titanic, foundational scholars I felt like a kid in a World Series locker room. Though it was nearly fifteen years before I presented my first paper at an ACIS gathering, all of the chapters that follow began life in that venue.

Some years later, I began working as a staff writer for the Irish American Cultural Institute, an anomalous organization that lat-

Introduction

er decided its future lay in New Jersey, a move I was not willing to make. But Ireland had its hooks into me, and since 1996 I have been employed by the University of St. Thomas as managing director, and now director, of its Center for Irish Studies. In other words, I have been lucky enough to spend most of my adult life working in or near the world of Irish Studies.

At a very deep level, I truly do believe that all good writing is personal: some of the works discussed here are old friends, and a few of these books were transformative.

From a historian's perspective, autobiographies and memoirs can be problematic sources. From a literary perspective they are frequently irresistible. The project of this book—an attempt to track the shifting meanings of Irishness in America, as those meanings found expression in memoirs—is a topic that emerges from a history of its own. One part of that history is the rise of autobiography itself as a subject of study. Memoirs, with which we are now awash, were a stepchild in the formal study of literature until very recent times. In terms of ethnic autobiography, Alex Haley's *Roots*—not coincidentally, a book that appeared in 1976, the year of America's great retrospective of the bicentennial—and the television series that followed, was in every sense a game-changer.[1]

Another and perhaps even more basic part of the background to this book is the arrival of Irish America as a subject deserving of attention in its own right—not an afterthought or appendage to Ireland, but an integral part of its history and culture. The rise of a diasporic model within Irish Studies is a wholly good thing and likewise a recent development; it was not that long ago that discussing Irish America pretty much meant recycling whatever the sociologist Andrew Greeley had written. One of the scholars I met at that first meeting in Chicago was Charles Fanning, who was just setting out on his study *The Irish Voice in America*.[2] When Fanning received one of his many honors for his scholarship a few years ago,

1. Alex Haley, *Roots: The Saga of an American Family* (New York: Doubleday, 1976).
2. Charles Fanning, *The Irish Voice in America: 250 Years of Irish-American Fiction* (Lexington: University Press of Kentucky, 1990).

the citation stated that every research act in Irish-American literature begins with his work. This book, which I have presumed to
dedicate to Charlie, is no exception.

As the historian Patrick Blessing has observed, there came a
point when the story of the Irish in America became "the story of
Americans of Irish descent."[3] There seems to be a consensus that
the transformative point in that process was right around the turn
of the twentieth century, which is where this study begins. The
chapters that follow appear in loose chronological order, ending
with a look at the recent flourishing of memoirs involving present-day "return" trips to Ireland. (The quotes around "return" are
intentional: many of those travelers had never stepped foot in Ireland before.) With the exception of three of the memoirists writing
about genealogical searches in chapter 5, every author discussed
here was born in the United States. Frank McCourt, whose autobiography is the subject of chapter 7, was at the time of his death
in 2009 almost certainly the most famous Irish person in America;
but he was born in Brooklyn, and McCourt's youth in Limerick was
filled with longing for America, a clear instance of the "divided
heart" that I call out in this volume's subtitle. Indeed, one way or
another, we can discern a psychic or emotional split in the heart of
all these autobiographers. There are many sorts of rivenness: the
sadness that lies under the humor (Jackie Gleason's *Honeymooners*,
discussed in chapter 4, is a textbook case); a disconnection from
one's own past, as the genealogical researchers report in chapter
5; the "larking" of step dancer Barbara Mullen, side by side with
a hardscrabble struggle to survive in chapter 2; and the psychic
homelessness running under the surface of so many narratives of
return in the closing chapter.

Of course, dividedness is usually where autobiography begins:
every autobiographer's project is to make sense of the warring parts

3. Patrick J. Blessing, "Irish Emigration to the United States: An Overview," in
The Irish in America: Emigration, Assimilation, and Impact, ed. P. J. Drudy, Irish Studies 4
(Cambridge: Cambridge University Press, 1985), 31. Blessing identifies that point as
1920; I would contend it is several decades earlier.

Introduction

of the self. I happen to hold the opinion that the autobiographical impulse is fundamentally a religious one, in the sense that its purpose is to make meaning; one reason we have lately been living in "the age of memoir" might be precisely a rejection of the postmodern assumption that our lives are constructed and arbitrary.

Although the extent to which we choose to display our ethnic affiliation is, for most white Americans, a self-determined matter, that identity isn't generally something we get to choose. Elsewhere, I have written of Irish-American memoirists that they are "certain that being Irish in America conveys something distinctive—even if they are not always clear what that distinctiveness is, nor necessarily pleased when they find out."[4] Reminders of Ireland are everywhere in popular culture, from the bins of Celtic CDs at the Target store to the franchised authenticity of the Irish Pub Company,[5] and if your name is Murphy, O'Rourke, or O'Neill, it is all but impossible to go twenty-four hours without someone commenting on your Irishness. How odd, though, that America's attention to Ireland and Irishness endures long after ethnic and religious out-marriage became the norm; seven or eight decades after the group ceased to be a meaningful voting bloc; and a full half-century after all but a few of the urban neighborhoods that sustained Irish ethnicity were abandoned for the suburbs. The very superficiality of such markers of an identity is quite possibly part of what contributes to their attraction.

A strong statement of such attraction appears near the start of Dan Barry's *Pull Me Up*, discussed in chapter 9, where the author writes of his fascination with the music of the Clancy Brothers's folk songs while a pre-teen in 1970s Long Island, and asks, "But why did we sing them?" He asks himself if it were to "help us in piecing together how we came to be, and how we came to be here on Long

4. James Silas Rogers, "Introduction," in *Extended Family: Essays on Being Irish American from "New Hibernia Review"* (Chester Springs, Pa.: Dufour Editions, 2013), 12.

5. The Irish Pub Company, http://irishpubcompany.com/, is a spinoff of the Guinness brewing conglomerate. Its website claims that it has designed more than seven hundred pubs in fifty-three countries, all of which purport to be authentic.

4

Introduction

Island, in a place called Deer Park." It is not a rhetorical question: helping to piece together the narrative of our lives is exactly the purpose of autobiography. Ethnically inflected autobiographies are especially good at describing that process. The general trajectory of the books discussed here reveals that, the further away the writers are from the immigrant generations, the greater their interiority. Irishness in America becomes a sort of found object, abstracted from its contexts, and the challenge of discerning its meaning turns inward, a matter of personal reflection.

Thus, it is helpful to keep in mind the distinction made by Kathleen Brogan in *Cultural Haunting: Ghosts and Ethnicity in Recent American Literature*—a book that, by the way, pays no attention at all to Irish-American writing—between "ethnographers" and "heirs."[6] Ethnographers, in this schema, seek to describe characteristics and the stuff of a cohering subculture (food, clothing, holiday rituals, and the like) in which the author is immersed by birth or by a commitment to research. Heirs, on the other hand, engage in a more active process of, as it were, inventing an ethnic identity out of scattered knowledge and interrupted traditions (or nakedly constructed ones, such as *Kiss Me, I'm Irish!* buttons). This book is about heirs.

In some cases, my goal in this volume has been merely to call attention to a book that is deserving of renewed attention, or even of attention, period. There are some fascinating works waiting to be discovered, none more worthy of a second look than Barbara Mullen's *Life Is My Adventure* of 1937 (chapter 2), which to my mind just begs to be reissued. But there are other jewels referenced here: Donald Hayne's quirky but oddly fascinating spiritual autobiography *Batter My Heart* (1963); Andrew Sheehan's *Chasing the Hawk* (2001); and Dan Barry's *Pull Me Up* (2004), about which I claim in chapter 9 that it may be the first great memoir of suburbia. There are also some dreadful books: it was almost a penance to read the

6. Kathleen Brogan, chap. 1, "Haunted Tales of Heirs and Ethnographers," in *Cultural Haunting: Ghosts and Ethnicity in Recent American Literature* (Charlottesville: University of Virginia Press), 1–29.

5

Introduction

clumsy scribblings of boxers and ballplayers for the first chapter, and even worse, to slog through the pious bilge in the priests' autobiographies discussed in chapter 5. Winston Churchill once said that no man ever wrote a boring autobiography; he obviously hadn't read many lives of priests. And yet these inept memoirs, too, speak to the larger inquiry that knits together all of these chapters: the task of understanding the various meanings of Irishness in America.

Almost everything ever written about the Irish identity in America concludes that it has rested on four elements: Catholicism; the Democratic Party (especially in its labor wing); an attachment to urban neighborhoods; and involvement in nationalist struggle in Ireland. On the whole, I think that these four claims are accurate. It is noteworthy, though, that two of these themes, politics in Ireland and politics in America, are missing completely in the books discussed in this study. Or perhaps that is not completely surprising. Reflection is the engine that drives memoir, and political life rarely fosters reflection.

As for the other two badges of Irish-American identity—Catholicism and city life—they are without doubt present, though sometimes in a deflected way. The neighborhoods of urban America shaped the lives of many of these autobiographers. Mill towns and the waterfront were the first homes of the athletes discussed in the opening chapter. Barbara Mullen and Michael Patrick MacDonald (in chapters 2 and 8) each came out of Boston's Southie and, though separated by sixty years, their stories open an enticing window on that enclave of Irish isolation in the United States. In chapter 3, Joseph Mitchell's project of evoking the texture and exoticism of old New York necessarily involves drawing portraits of the Irish, including a loving account of McSorley's saloon. The Irish become a figure in the carpet in his New York. In chapter 4, which examines the Irish subtexts of *The Honeymooners*, I tried to show how the comedian Jackie Gleason reproduced the scarcity and frustrations of his Brooklyn childhood in the classic 1950s situation comedy. And it seems, too, that at least the memory of urban America still lurks in the family memories of David Beers and Dan Barry when they cast their autobiographical eye over their own primal landscapes of American suburbia.

Catholicism also percolates through these accounts. Obviously, it is an inescapable presence in the lives of the priests. Yet, despite the confessional identity of the Irish—the widespread, if not wholly accurate, presumption that Irish means Catholic and Catholic means Irish—religion is little in evidence in the earlier books (and for better or worse, the Protestant Irish voice is missing altogether). The more surprising, then, that later writers appear attuned to what has sometimes been called "the Catholic imagination."[7] Ways of perceiving the world and of structuring reality that can be traced to Catholic origins inform the works discussed in the later chapters. In chapter 6, I discuss a number of writers who have undertaken genealogical research and who end up shifting from the realm of fact to that of imagination: it is not too great a stretch to think of that move as a leap of faith, a "conviction of things unseen." Michael Patrick MacDonald adapts the figure of the guardian angel to make sense of his harrowing childhood in South Boston. The suburbanites looking back in chapter 9 recall the physical space of their spanking-new parish churches as imparting continuity and meaning to a seemingly placeless environment. Probably nothing has altered the psychic landscape of Irish America so thoroughly as the phenomenon of mass tourism, allowing literally millions of individuals to (supposedly) come face-to-face with the land of their ancestors. In chapter 10, which discusses the phenomenon of "roots trips," several authors clearly construe their trips back to Ireland as pilgrimages.

I might remark another continuity threading through the works discussed here: so many of these Irish-American autobiographers report feeling like outsiders, though their sense of exclusion operates on many different levels. It need hardly be said that the

7. The term was introduced by Andrew M. Greeley, *The Catholic Imagination* (Berkeley: University of California Press, 2000).

Introduction

charge that the Irish were not quite reputable has a long pedigree, both at home and abroad; it is striking that a concern for respectability has continued to evolve alongside the larger assimilation of the Irish. One thinks of the visceral reaction that McCourt's portrayal of poverty evoked; of how Jackie Gleason's alter ego Ralph Kramden felt the shame about being "just a bus driver"; of the fetishized cleanliness of suburbia; of those good little boys who grew up to enter the seminary. And there other, more interior sorts of outsiderhood, expressed in a sense of spiritual homelessness and of being deprived of one's own history. It does seem as if the genealogical impulse that (in the broadest sense) lies behind so much Irish-American autobiography has much do with the feeling of being on the outside looking in.

Irish-American identity is surely not a fixed commodity. It is nothing if not adaptive. Irish identity in America has largely moved out of the quantifiable—census returns, membership in churches or fraternal organizations, voting behavior, and the like—and into the slippery realm of the imagination and the psyche. But I remain convinced that, despite all the forces of homogenization (and all the ersatz markers of Irish wheeled out every St. Patrick's Day), there is still a distinct Irish identity in America. Memoir and autobiography provide essential windows on what that identity comprises. It is my hope that the chapters that follow persuade readers that the story of the Irish in America is in some ways the story of an "ethnic fade" that never quite happened.

1

Sporting Gentlemen

The Memoirs of John L. Sullivan, James J. Corbett, and Connie Mack

At its emotional core, Irish literature almost always returns to binaries, dualisms, and contradictions. Whether at home or abroad, Irish life seems to rest on one fault line after another. It is easy to compile a list of such fissures: for starters, the dual traditions of Gaelic and English; the happy-go-lucky comic versus the brooding pessimist; authoritarianism against a taste for anarchy; piety locked in battle with cynicism; home and exile; and immigrant or emigrant, which in the United States is followed by the unending negotiation of "Irish or Irish-American?"

The Irish-American community, during the closing decades of the nineteenth century and the opening decades of the twentieth, moved back and forth across another such divide: a complicated evolution of class and status that came to be known in shorthand as the clash of the "shanty Irish" and the "lace curtain Irish." On the one hand, the Irish aspired to respectability, good citizenship, responsibility, and self-control; on the other, they were emerging from the near anarchy of the years that followed the famine

Sporting Gentlemen

immigration. One highly public site in which Irish Americans, eager to be accepted and recognized, set out to prove their all-American credentials was in the arena of sport.

And what athletes they were! As the nineteenth century wound down, the Irish were as visible in sports as African Americans are in our day. Traditional Irish games, such as hurling or handball, had only a spotty presence in the New World (or had not crossed the ocean in the first place; the Gaelic Athletic Association, so central to the "revival" of these games, was not founded until 1884). But the Irish dominated early baseball, track and field events, and most conspicuously, prizefighting.[1]

In 1888, the poet and littérateur John Boyle O'Reilly published a high-minded defense of athleticism entitled *The Ethics of Boxing and Manly Sport*.[2] The very idea that O'Reilly would write a book about a sport that confirmed all of the public's worst fears about the Irish abounds with irony. Whereas the typical boxer of the day was presumed to be intemperate, uncouth, corrupt, and violent, O'Reilly was, at that point, the most respected Irishman in Boston. He served as almost the default orator at Irish social events and was a bright light in the literary and cultural world of his adopted home. As the editor of the diocesan paper *The Pilot* and a friend of Longfellow and Howells, O'Reilly embodied Irish-American gentility and social aspirations. His literary career bridged the Irish community and the world of high culture.[3] After dramatically escaping an Australian

---

1. There is a certain amount of bombast in much of the literature on the Irish in American sports, although there are also some outstanding biographical studies. For a helpful short survey, see Ralph C. Wilcox, "The Shamrock and the Eagle: Irish Americans and Sport in the Nineteenth Century," in *Ethnicity and Sport in North American History and Culture*, ed. George Eisen and David K. Wiggins (Westport, Conn.: Greenwood Press, 1994), 55–74.

2. John Boyle O'Reilly, *Ethics of Boxing and Manly Sport* (Boston: Ticknor and Sons, 1888).

3. On O'Reilly, see Conor Johnston, "John Boyle O'Reilly (1844–1890)," *Encyclopedia of the Irish in America*, ed. Michael Glazier (Notre Dame: University of Notre Dame Press, 1999), 753–55. Unsurprisingly, O'Reilly's early life as a revolutionary and as the hero of a daring prison escape has attracted much more attention from

prison colony where he had been sent for his revolutionary activities, O'Reilly had found his home and fame in America, and he fully embraced nineteenth-century American patriotism. His boxing book is in all ways an American treatise; O'Reilly boasts of American manliness and vigor, delivered in the spirit of moral uplift. But unsurprisingly, he also finds many occasions to praise specifically Irish contributions to the cult of athleticism. His insistence that prizefighting could also be ennobling amounted to making the same claim for the Irish, who, he asserts, are blessed with natural athleticism. He goes so far as to make the unvarnished claim that "there is no branch of athletics in which Irishmen, or the sons of Irishmen, do not hold first place in all the world."[4] The boast is subject to debate but, on the whole, was closer to true than many would realize.

This chapter will look at memoirs by three of those "sons of Irishmen." Their books open a window on this transitional era. John L. Sullivan, the last bare-knuckle champion and the first champion of the modern era, was born in Boston in 1858; he was a genuine superstar, an irresistible outsider in an age when the idea of celebrity was being refined and cultivated in the media. Connie Mack (whose real name was Cornelius McGillicuddy), baseball's "Tall Tactician," was born near Worcester in 1862; in his public life, he raised respectability to an art form. Boxer James J. Corbett, widely known as "Gentleman Jim" and the man who took the title from Sullivan, was born in San Francisco in 1866. His role in Irish-American life is a complex one, crossing both sides of the social gulf.

The not-so-hidden subtext of each of their autobiographies matches that of O'Reilly's defense of pugilism: an assertion that, despite the poverty of their youths and the rough edges of their sporting lives, they were gentlemen. They understood, too, that as public figures, they were taking on the burden of representation for their ethnic group; Sullivan would write on one occasion that

---

biographers than his later life as a civic leader and littérateur; see, for example, A. G. Evans, *Fanatic Heart: A Life of John Boyle O'Reilly, 1844–1890* (Nedlands: University of Western Australia Press, 1999).

4. O'Reilly, *Ethics of Boxing*, 173.

Sporting Gentlemen

"My father and mother were Irish, and I always aim at upholding the honor of the Irish people, who are a brave race."[5]

As literature, these memoirs are far from artful. Mack's is particularly wooden. They are in almost all ways the stories of the authors' lives in sports and not explorations of their private lives. Nor is it likely there could be interiority; even to call them autobiographies is a stretch, as the athletes themselves may not actually have written them. Sullivan's *Life and Reminiscences* appears ghostwritten, with a great deal of it comprising reprints of press clippings.[6] Corbett's *The Roar of the Crowd* (first published in serial form in the *Saturday Evening Post*) is easily the most interesting of the three books, in part because it does show the hand of its author—though internal cues indicate it was written by dictation and revised on the fly.[7] Mack's *My 66 Years in the Big Leagues* appeared in 1950;[8] according to his biographer, Norman Macht, Mack himself may never have read his own ghostwritten autobiography.[9]

Yet it hardly matters. Any insights about the inner lives of the authors (or putative authors) found in these books reveal themselves by indirection. Men who spent their professional lives in staging highly public athletic contests would naturally be inclined to approach life-writing as if it, too, were a performance. It is worth noting that the boxers also moved seamlessly into a life on the stage, and although Connie Mack never went on the vaudeville circuit, many of the stars whom he played with or managed routinely did so in the off-season; despite the complaints of purists, baseball has always included an element of show business.[10]

5. Quoted in John R. Betts, "John Boyle O'Reilly and the American Paideia," *Éire-Ireland* 2, no. 4 (Winter 1967): 36–52.

6. John L. Sullivan, *Life and Reminiscences of a 19th-Century Gladiator* (Boston: J. A. Hearn, 1892).

7. James J. Corbett, *The Roar of the Crowd: The Rise and Fall of a Champion* (New York: G. P. Putnams's Sons, 1925).

8. Connie Mack, *My Sixty-Six Years in the Big Leagues* (Mineola, N.Y.: Dover, 2009).

9. Norman L. Macht, *Connie Mack and the Early Years of Baseball* (Lincoln: University of Nebraska Press, 2007), 94.

10. See Ricard Pioreck, "Baseball and Vaudeville in the Development of Popular

But it would be wrong to assume that the rowdiness and egotism of the earlier day were completely disowned or denied, or that these qualities did not also appeal to newly respectable Irish Americans at the time; the Irish exaltation of personality goes way back.

We should be on guard against presentism as we consider these texts. Their solemn professions of propriety may appear quaint to us, and our contemporary tastes are likely to find the flamboyant personality and raciness of Sullivan more attractive than the bourgeois figures who succeeded him. Faced with a prude like Connie Mack, we incline to sniff out repression and, by extension, to conclude that his decorousness includes a measure of covering-up and hypocrisy.

In fact, men like Sullivan, Corbett, and Mack were well aware of their capacity for disreputable conduct. They knew their "dark sides" full well and how recently they and their families were presumed to be outcasts. The factories, docks, and construction sites where they had worked as young men, or in which their fathers worked, were brutal, violent places, as were the saloons and brawls that comprised much of the social milieu. But they believed that they had a "better self" as well and carried the conviction that when in the public eye it was necessary to perform that better self. Manners, social codes, and the expectations of a gentleman were a way of regulating what they considered their own worst instincts—in a word, their sinfulness. In these books and in their lives they may have been "performing respectability"—but just because it was a performance, that doesn't mean they didn't believe it.

The internal clash of cultures in Irish America saw a mythic enactment in the famous match between John L. Sullivan and James J. Corbett in 1892. John V. Kelleher, who wrote as intelligently as anyone ever has about Irish America, opens his 1961 article "Irishness in America" precisely by discussing the Corbett-Sullivan bout. The transition from Sullivan to Corbett provided a perfect symbol

---

Culture in the United States, 1880–1930," in *The Cooperstown Symposium on Baseball and American Culture, 1999* (Jefferson, N.C.: McFarland, 2000), 83–100.

of the transition that Kelleher's father called the great "sorting out" of the Irish, when the sons of Irishmen "walked easily into jobs their fathers could never have dreamed of."[11] As the century drew to a close, Sullivan, Corbett, and Mack, along with tens of thousands of other such sons and daughters of Irishmen, participated in a massive upward spike in Irish economic and social advancement. Kelleher quite specifically pinpoints 1904 to 1905 as the tipping point when the Irish community lost the last of its roughest edges. Sullivan, he writes, "was only eight years older than Corbett, but they stood on either side of a gulf of history neither their imagination nor their experience could bridge."[12]

Boxing has always melded sophistication with brutishness; its ringside fans in tuxedoes assert as much at every title match. In the nineteenth century, that brutishness carried a distinctly Irish cast. The sport's most prominent practitioner (and the recipient of effulgent praise in O'Reilly's book), John L. Sullivan, was a man who—when not defending his championship—earned and squandered several fortunes, drank champagne by the bucket, left his wife to live openly with a chorus girl, and generally served as a walking affront to Victorian morality. In his drinking days, the champion routinely announced his entry into any saloon by striding up to the bar, bringing his fist down with a crash, and declaring "My name is John L Sullivan and I can lick any son-of-a-bitch in the house!"[13]

When, in 1979, a publisher spotted his *Life and Reminiscences of a 19th-Century Gladiator* in public domain and reissued it, the memoir was retitled *I Can Lick Any Sonofabitch in the House*[14]—a celebration of loutishness that would have horrified O'Reilly and, for that matter,

11. John V. Kelleher, "Irish in America," in *Selected Writings of John V. Kelleher on Ireland and Irish America*, ed. Charles F. Fanning (Carbondale: Southern Illinois University Press, 2002), 128.

12. Kelleher, "Irish in America," 151.

13. The flamboyant Sullivan has attracted dozens of biographers, beginning in his own lifetime. A masterful study is Michael T. Isenberg, *John L. Sullivan and His America* (Urbana: University of Illinois Press, 1988).

14. Sullivan, *I Can Lick Any Sonofabitch in the House*, ed. Gilbert Odd (London: Proteus, 1979).

Sullivan himself when he was on his good behavior. Again, the Irish gift for contradiction leaps out. The fact that the same book could appear under two titles, one evoking classic courage and the other hooliganism, is, in a way, the point: Sullivan knew that certain behaviors were unacceptable, but at the same time he delighted in his own transgressiveness and knew that the public delighted in it, too.

The authors were much in the public eye at this moment of "sorting out," though Mack's longevity as a manager (more than fifty years; it helps to own the ball club) kept him a public figure for much longer than the two prizefighters. All three grew up in and, in Sullivan's case, became the celebrated exemplar of the old Irish-American community of rough-and-tumble street life, part of what Kelleher describes as "a huge fund of poor, unskilled, cheap, almost infinitely exploitable labor . . . [that was expended] with a callousness now hard to comprehend."[15] And all three—in their well-constructed public personae and in these texts—deliberately shed the association with disreputable origins. To a considerable extent each approached his autobiography as an exercise in performing respectability

Aware of John L.'s raffish reputation, O'Reilly's defense of boxing had nonetheless proudly noted that Sullivan, by insisting on Marquis of Queensbury rules, effectively put an end to the bare-knuckle era. "In America," he wrote, "Sullivan's example has done much to bring glove contests into professional practice; and when the man's faults are rehearsed, it is only fair that this should be remembered."[16] His roundhouse style of fighting remained a matter of raw strength, but it was civilized.

Sullivan announces in the early pages of *Life and Reminiscences* that his goal is to show that he can hold his own in respectable society:

I wish to show to my readers and to the public in general, that there is one, who, while in the line of a professional pugilist and boxer, is quite capable of informing them through the medium of this book,

15. Kelleher, "Irish in America," 151.
16. Quoted in Betts, "John Boyle O'Reilly and the American Paideia," 44.

that he is gifted with ordinary ability, and is conscious of being something more than a pugilist. I want them also to understand that, while
not of an egotistical nature, I have a fair amount of common sense,
and, with a Boston public school education, can give an intelligent
opinion on almost any subject, and conduct myself as a gentleman in
any company.[17]

The word "gentleman" is key. In the late nineteenth century, to be
a gentleman entailed a number of virtues: intelligence, certainly,
but also integrity, well-regulated emotion, respect for women, du-
tifulness, and, highly important, an avoidance of rough language;
in a word, manners. Irish Catholic respectability stressed further
elements: religious observance coupled with an exalted view of
the priesthood and a "filial piety," which often meant a home life
focused on an idealized version of motherhood. Less familiar to
present-day sensibilities, the Victorian ideal of gentlemanliness
to which the athletes aspired unapologetically involved breeding,
as well. John Ruskin had written, "The essence of a gentleman, is
what the word says, that he comes from a pure *gens*, or is perfectly bred."[18] Sullivan, Corbett, and Mack's affectionate portrayals of
their parents amount to more than sentiment; they are a claim of
the social, cultural, and genetic legitimacy that—however much it
may have been thwarted in Irish history—was now allowed to display itself in America.

Sullivan says little about his mother, who was from Athlone,
County Westmeath, though he does give her credit for his physical
stature. Admitting that he "has been noticed for size or strength"
and that "my father was a small man" (only five-three), he goes on
to note that "My mother was of fair size, weighing about one hundred and eighty pounds, and some have given the credit to her."[19]

In the first chapter, Sullivan offers these enticing sentences
about his adolescence: "After leaving the Public School I went to

17. Sullivan, *Life and Reminiscences*, 21.

18. David Cody, "The Gentleman," *The Victorian Web*, http://www.victorianweb
.org/history/gentleman.html.

19. Sullivan, *Life and Reminiscences*, 21.

Comer's Commercial College, and attended about one year. From that I went to Boston College, Harrison Avenue, where I studied about sixteen months. It was the desire of my parents to have me study for the priesthood, but it was not mine."[20] Not a lot of evidence, but that simple equation—it was their desire "but it was not mine"— suggests he was not merely a strong boy, but a strong-willed boy.

Connie Mack completed grammar school, but at age nine he began summer work in a Brookfield cotton mill, working twelve-hour shifts. At age thirteen, he started to work in a shoe factory and rose to the position of assistant foreman by the time he was twenty-one. His baseball career was confined to amateur play. Financial disaster struck when the shoe factory closed in 1884, but fortunately, Mack was offered a chance to play professionally for the Connecticut State League. But first, Mack did what any good boy would do and consulted his mother (though as the region was in the midst of a paralyzing recession, one has to wonder what his economic choices really were). Nonetheless, he did seek her advice, which was cautionary regarding the rough characters he was likely to encounter. Here is the reported exchange: "'Promise me one thing,' she said. 'Promise me that you won't let them get you into bad habits. I've brought you up to be a good boy. Promise me that you won't drink.' I promised her, and that promise I shall keep to the end of my life."[21] Mack always urged his players to be kind to their own mothers. His loyalty was repaid: when his first wife died of tuberculosis only five years after their marriage, Mack's mother raised his three children while Connie lived the itinerant life of a professional athlete and manager.

Corbett's *The Roar of the Crowd* repeatedly asserts his lifelong dedication to his parents. After attaining success, he pays off their mortgage, and late in the book the champion takes great delight in taking his mother back to Ireland. He presents his family as exemplary: "That there was harmony in our family, and respect paid to

20. Ibid., 31.
21. Mack, *My Sixty-Six Years*, 17.

our parents, is evident from the fact that for the six years I was a bank clerk I gave my monthly salary to my mother each pay day."[22] Corbett was indeed a new kind of fighter—not the profligate, throwing his money away, but the responsible saver. It should surprise no one that his mother, too, had another dream for her son: that he become a priest. (He was deliberately given the name "James" for the uncle back in Ireland who had a vocation.)

Corbett's memoir also presents his father as deeply divided with regard to his son's profession, simultaneously ill-at-ease and proud of him, enacting the tension between the promises of security and the promises of public adulation.[23] The young Corbett got plenty of messages about respectability at home. He records an exchange a few weeks before his first big fight with local slugger Joe Choinyski in which his father earnestly says, "Jim my boy, you know how proud I am of you working in the bank. Your mother and your sisters are, too. Boxing in the club's all right, but the bank people won't like fighting in the street, and I wouldn't have you lose that job for anything in the world."[24] True to the stereotype, a few pages later, when the elder Corbett learns that his son has licked two tough fellows he triumphantly proclaims, "To hell with the bank."[25]

Corbett was entirely conscious of the cultural identifications he carried into the ring with him. Of his first fight with Choinyski, he writes that there were "more than just the two fighters in the ring," and lists the antagonists as also including the California Club versus the Olympic, professional sport versus amateur, Jew versus Gentile, labor versus capital, and "Golden Gate Ave, (his neighborhood) versus Hayes Street (mine)." He expands on the dimension of labor versus capital by adding that "Choinyski was a candy-puller at the time and all the factory people were cheering for him, while

22. Corbett, *Roar of the Crowd*, 19. Mack, incidentally, reports doing the same thing with his wages from a shoe factory; Mack, *My Sixty-six Years*, 10.

23. The surprisingly good biopic *Gentleman Jim* (1942, directed by Raoul Walsh) and starring Errol Flynn as Corbett, captures this tension well.

24. Corbett, *Roar of the Crowd*, 39.

25. Ibid., 41.

my bosses at the bank and the wealthy business men who belonged to the Olympic were pulling for me."[26] In setting up these dichotomies, Corbett situates himself in a political context that would have been recognized by his readers. *The Roar of the Crowd* appeared a mere five years after the Palmer Raids: when he speaks of labor versus capital, Jew versus Gentile, he is letting us know on which side he lines up.

And he surely knew what he represented when he was matched with Sullivan. Without saying as much, his emphasis on a "scientific" boxing is a pointed renunciation of the old lumbering brawn of the earlier generation. As Kelleher writes, Corbett "was a prophetic figure: slim, deft, witty, looking like a proto-Ivy Leaguer with his pompadour, his fresh intelligent face, his well-cut young man's clothes. He was, as it were, the paradigm of all those young Irish Americans about to make the grade."[27]

Throughout *The Roar of the Crowd*, Corbett takes pains to describe the fight promoters and referees as "gentlemen"; when he refuses to fight Jake Kilrain after discovering that the New Orleans businessman who was the referee had bet on his opponent, the dispute is characterized as the stuff of a drawing room:

"I've no doubt but that you stand pretty well here and are a gentleman."

"I certainly am a gentleman, Sir!" he came back at me.

"That's fine." I took him up quickly "and since you're a gentleman, if one of the principals in this contest objected to you being referee, you, being such a gentleman, would naturally resign."

"I certainly would," he replied.

"I'm glad of that, Sir, also that you are a gentleman," I declared, "Because I happen to object to your being referee."[28]

It is, of course, hard to believe that this Socratic dialogue faithfully renders the discussion of bare-chested fighters on a barge in New Orleans. But Corbett takes care to cultivate the image of rationality.

26. Ibid., 65.   27. Kelleher, "Irish in America," 152.

28. Corbett, *Roar of the Crowd*, 104.

Sporting Gentlemen

Nowhere is his propriety better displayed than in an incident when the young Corbett spent a night in the company of the Great John L., several years before the two were to meet in their famous title match. Sullivan was in San Francisco, touring with the melodrama *Honest Hearts and Willing Hands*, in which—notwithstanding his reputation for dissipation and bombast—he played a humble blacksmith compelled to defend the reputation of a young woman. Corbett, who had just agreed to fight the black heavyweight Peter Jackson (Sullivan refused to fight blacks) joins in Sullivan's entourage. There is strategy involved from the beginning: Sullivan knows that he will have to face Corbett eventually and tries to impress the young boxer with his roughness. Corbett, in turn, seeks to display his unflappability.

John L. makes his signature declaration at every bar they enter; Corbett does not drink. Late in the night, Sullivan repeats the performance in a famous, upscale watering-hole called Mat Hogan's, where, as the abstemious Corbett tells it, the champion

once more banged his fist on the counter and made the old boast, "I can lick any blankety-blank in the world," this time looking at me with a particularly ferocious and contemptuous glance.

I was pretty well worked up by this time. This doesn't mean I lost my temper, for, as a rule, I sometimes get excited over trivial things, but am very cool in crises, no matter how resentful I may feel.

I looked him right in the eye and said, "Mr. Sullivan, you have made that remark several times in my presence tonight. You are the champion of the world everybody is supposed to think you can whip any —— in the world. But I am in the same profession as yourself and it's hardly courteous, and I don't want you to make that remark in my presence again!"[29]

In Corbett's version, Sullivan "listens to reason"—that is Corbett's precise phrase—and a professional respect ensues.

Early baseball is not generally considered the Irish specialty that prizefighting is, though Jerrold Casway's work has gone far to

29. Ibid., 120–21.

prove there was "an emerald age."[30] But baseball may in fact be a better embodiment of the Irish-American experience. At the end of the nineteenth century, the institution of baseball shared many of the concerns, and aspirations, of the American Irish. Gambling, liquor, brawling, and venereal disease had all been associated individually and collectively with ballplayers. As the new century approached, for baseball—as for the Irish—a rocky economic past appeared to be coming to an end. The twentieth century promised previously unattainable prosperity.

And with this new good fortune, the institution of baseball likewise sought to cast off an unsavory reputation. When Ban Johnson established the American League in 1901, the new circuit consciously sought to present a more sanitized and socially acceptable pastime. For example, the introduction of reserved box seats, reducing the likelihood of rubbing shoulders with a rough element, was a deliberate attempt to court a more genteel clientele. To find a paragon of respectability to take up the reins of one of his new clubs, the Philadelphia Athletics, Johnson had to look no further than his friend Connie Mack.

Mack had risen rapidly in professional baseball. Known to be a young man of exceptionally clean habits, he had nonetheless been well able to cope with the rough-and-tumble of the baseball of that era. In his playing days he was not above bending or ignoring the rules. As a catcher, he was known to be adept at interfering with a swung bat, to have mastered mimicking the sound of a tipped ball with his teeth, and in a famous maneuver, to put frozen and thus very dead baseballs into play when the opposition was at bat. Perhaps his most startling departure from conventionality was Mack's participation in the player's revolt of 1890. His motivation appears to have been chiefly economic, but even as a young player Mack stood apart from the devil-may-care attitude of the majority of ball players. He was planning a lifelong career in the game.

---

30. Jerrold Casway, *Ed Delahanty in the Emerald Age of Baseball* (Notre Dame: University of Notre Dame Press, 2004).

Sporting Gentlemen

Despite the reported promise to his mother, Mack was not a strict teetotaler, but in public he consistently played one. (Mack's first biographer, the sportswriter Fred Lieb, makes a point of showing that as a young player, on one occasion, Mack actually bought a round of drinks.) He was on record as opposed to Prohibition. Yet he clearly disapproved of alcohol. As a manager, players who drank too much did not receive lectures, but knew that the instant their drinking intruded upon their play, they would find themselves playing somewhere else soon. Mack was a devout Catholic who attended Mass every Sunday of his life and would invite players to attend with him. His daughter Mary joined the order of St. Joseph at Chestnut Hill, and as an owner he was lavish with passes to members of the Catholic clergy, to the point where it was said that every priest on the East Coast was an unofficial scout for the Athletics. And despite his reputation as a cheapskate, Mack was privately a very generous individual.

His disdain for vulgarity and rough language was famous. In a sappy treatise for young readers called *Connie Mack's Baseball Book*, the venerable manager took care to present the game in terms of personal conduct, advising rookies that they must "have good moral habits and self-control. You can have everything else that's needed to make the grade, but if you don't have good moral character you are not for the big leagues."[31]

Such platitudes did not begin or end with Connie Mack, but his particular gift was to create a public persona that embodied these virtues and, by his very presence, to impart dignity and propriety to a passionate game. Wilfrid Sheed once quipped that not swearing counts as the "pinnacle of virtue in baseball,"[32] and it was a virtue of which Mack stayed ever mindful. In 1925, he pronounced that

31. Mack, *Connie Mack's Baseball Book* (New York: Alfred A. Knopf, 1950), 50.
32. Wilfrid Sheed, "Mr. Mack and the Main Chance," in *The Ultimate Baseball Book*, ed. Daniel Okrent and Harris Lewine (Boston: Houghton Mifflin, 1979), 120.

There is room for gentlemen in any profession, and baseball is my profession. I will not allow my players to engage in any rough play.... I have told our boys that there can never be anything personal or malicious shouted at our opponents. We may face the charge that we are timid, but I will insist that my boys be gentlemen. They may kid back and forth, but I will not tolerate profanity, obscene language, or personal insults from my bench.[33]

Note, too, the paternalistic term "my boys"; Mack's "boys" in turn referred to him as "Mr. Mack." His formality was underscored by his practice of addressing players by their proper names: Robert, rather than Lefty Grove, Albert, rather than "Chief" Bender.

Mack's concern for the propriety and appearance of the game probably lay behind his innovative personnel policies of pursuing college stars for the Athletics, a deliberate attempt to upgrade the status of ballplayers. The illiterate country boy Shoeless Joe Jackson felt so out of place on what was called the "most highly educated ball club in history" that Mack had to release him. When the A's won the 1910 Series, the American League president declared the winners to be "dignified men in the best tradition of middle-class American values."[34] Personal reserve and humility—concepts foreign to Sullivan's well-crafted exaltation of personality—were a cherished aspect of this new dignity. So unobtrusive was Mack that it is said that when a civic holiday was declared in Philadelphia after the 1910 World Series, Mack rode a public streetcar to the mayor's office and went unrecognized.

Mack also made a conscious choice to wear civilian clothes rather than a uniform, and this decision prohibited him, under the rules of baseball, from venturing onto the field. To argue, which he rarely did, Mack would need to call the umpire over to his dugout. There were other managers of the day who elected to wear business dress rather than a uniform, but none who maintained the

33. Ted Davis, *Connie Mack: A Life in Baseball* (Bloomington, Ind.: iUniverse, 2000), 63.

34. Bruce Kuklick, *To Every Thing a Season: Shibe Park and Urban Philadelphia, 1909–1976* (Princeton: Princeton University Press, 1993), 38.

practice, and certainly none who kept it up for fifty years. His old-fashioned starched collars were so important to his public image that when they became unavailable commercially he had them privately manufactured.

What are we to make of this surprising, carefully cultivated formality? One explanation, surely, is that it bespoke an Irish Jansenistic fear of the flesh. An element of sexual jealousy undoubtedly contributed to the unwholesome reputation of nineteenth-century Irish ballplayers, precisely as it persists in popular attitudes toward black athletes today. Virtually all contemporary accounts of the colorful outfielder Michael "King" Kelly, for instance, refer to his wavy raven hair and describe him as "handsome," "manly," or some comparable term, and similar characterizations were the rule for his Irish contemporaries.[35] They were, it seems, playing out the Barry Lyndon figure of the Irish rake. That figure was refuted by the circumspect presence of Connie Mack: never an intemperate word, never a joshing nickname, never out of his starched collar.

The lives of Sullivan, Corbett, and Mack enact a movement away from self-created improvisation and performance and toward the living-out of a cultural script. Sullivan was an original, and for much of his life, a ruffian, who could nonetheless pretend sophistication. He may have been fond of invoking classical allusions—the *Gladiator* of his autobiography's title, for instance—but it is doubtful that many believed the sportswriter whom he proudly quotes as saying, "He was a very well-read man, and preferred any time to discuss Shakespeare, Gladstone or Parnell to talking fight."[36] His *Life and Reminiscences* speaks at length of his trip to England and his audience with the Prince of Wales, but the newspaper account he quotes makes a point of his casualness: "Neither the pugilist nor the prince were in the least bit stiff or formal in their manner, as they met and shook hands right heartily."[37] The two go on to chat

---

35. See, for example, Martin Appel, *Slide, Kelly, Slide: The Wild Life and Times of Mike "King" Kelly* (Lanham, Md.: Scarecrow Press, 1996).

36. Quoted in Isenberg, *John. L. Sullivan and His America*, 222.

37. Sullivan, *Life and Reminiscences*, 203.

about boxing like old pals; Sullivan asks the prince if he puts up his dukes much, anymore.

Corbett, in contrast, truly was a polished young man with a genuine sophistication. He read widely and attended the opera. Like Sullivan, Corbett appeared in melodramas, but he also played Hamlet in later life. Mack, a fiercely competitive ballplayer in his early years, went on to become a manager whose reputation for personal rectitude became more important than his baseball standing. His formal persona, coupled with his seniority, would in time come to eclipse or even excuse his baseball. The grand old man of baseball eventually came to be honored for his rectitude rather than his team's achievements: for instance, he was presented with the Bok Award for outstanding contributions to Philadelphia, named for Edward Bok of the *Ladies Home Journal*, and the Silver Arrow, the highest honor that could be bestowed by the Boy Scouts of America.

The cautious figure of Connie Mack might be thought of as emblematizing the end point of a progression in Irish-American life. That track, however, might be more complicated than the familiar tale of the "shanty Irish" turning into the "lace curtain Irish."

Neither the rectitude of Mack nor the faux gentility of Sullivan, and certainly not the proletarian battlegrounds out of which they emerged, defines Irish identity in America in our time. But from a later generation's viewpoint—a comfortable, affluent, and hyper-assimilated generation, we should note—there is something romantic about the notion of rough-and-tumble of the early years. Although the demographic of today's athletic talent pool has changed utterly, the old tension is almost literally enshrined in the example of Notre Dame. It is not coincidental that the university that stands second only to the election of John F. Kennedy as a symbol of Irish Catholic achievement in America proudly calls its teams the "Fighting Irish." John L. Sullivan's wish to have it both ways—to be able to lick any son of a bitch in the house, but also to take tea with the Prince of Wales—might, in fact, be a paradigmatic expression of Irishness in America. It is a convoluted, and often poorly articulated, identity in which dividedness lies at the heart.

2

Dancing Like Merry Hell

Barbara Mullen's *Life Is My Adventure*

When the American-born actress Barbara Mullen died in London on March 9, 1979, her brief *New York Times* obituary mentioned a number of her films, noted her recent appearance in *Arsenic and Old Lace* in London's West End, and adverted to her childhood in South Boston and her early appearances on stage at the age of three. Her film career included nineteen movies, starting with *Jeannie*, a 1941 romance in which she played the title character, and ending with the melodrama *The Very Edge* in 1963. Among her movies of particular Irish interest is the 1952 thriller *The Gentle Gunman*, featuring Dirk Bogarde as an IRA man on the run. In her stage career, Mullen created the character of Miss Marple in *Murder at the Vicarage* (1949). Despite these achievements, Mullen—like many actors who made a late transition into television—is best remembered today for her highly successful television role as Janet, the Scottish house-

An earlier version of this chapter appeared under the same title in *The Recorder: Journal of the American Irish Historical Society* 19, no. 2, and 20, no. 1 (Summer 2007), and is reprinted with permission.

keeper on the BBC comedy *Dr. Finlay's Casebook*, which ran from 1962 to 1967.[1]

But Mullen's legacy includes more than her life in the performing arts; she also left behind a remarkable memoir of growing up in an Irish-American community, *Life Is My Adventure*,[2] first published in the United States by Coward-McCann when Mullen was twenty-three years old. *Life Is My Adventure* requires a close look to be appreciated; the triteness of its title and the naïve voice of its author in the pages that follow make it easy to jump to the conclusion that the book is mere juvenilia. On a closer reading, Mullen's memoir merits a contemporary reader's attention at several levels. As a rare first-person view of the history of Irish music in America; as a portrait of Irish-American urban poverty before and during the Depression; and, finally, as a sometimes disturbing account of a young woman's coming to voice against an enforced silence, Mullen's unaffected story makes a major contribution to the literature of ethnic Irish America.

Begun shortly after its young author had landed on Inis Mór, the largest of the three Aran Islands, in order to reunite with her father, much of *Life Is My Adventure* reads as a picaresque account of growing up in an eccentric household. The Mullen household in South Boston, dominated by her hard-bitten mother, who ran a busy saloon during Prohibition, was, at best, a tumultuous one; a patched-together, amorphous household that included greenhorn immigrants and such colorful characters as Lady Biddy, an aged woman who is rumored to possess the gift of laying on curses as well as an undeniable thirst. The memoir's few reviewers at the time of publication focused on the outlandishness of the milieu:

1. "Barbara Mullen, 64, An Actress; First Appeared on the Stage at 3," *New York Times*, March 10, 1979; obituary, *Daily Telegraph*, March 10, 1979. Mullen's films and television roles are described in numerous online sources; particularly useful here has been the *New York Times All Movie Guide* found at http://movies.nytimes.com/pages/movies/index.html. For Mullen's films with Irish content, see Kevin Rockett, *The Irish Filmography* (Dublin: Red Mountain Press, 1996).

2. Barbara Mullen, *Life Is My Adventure* (New York: Coward-McCann, 1937).

Dancing Like Merry Hell

the *New Statesman* praised the memoir's "fun and high spirits,"[3] and the *New York Times* offered the assessment that Mullen's story "is all happy-go-lucky-helter-skelter, spontaneous. Although it touches privation and sadness 'Life is my Adventure' is conducive to light enjoyment rather than to feeling or thought."[4]

Mullen herself described the circumstances of composing her memoir as a matter of lucky chance. Her father, Pat Mullen, with her older brother P.J., had returned to the Aran Islands after separating from her mother. Mullen's secret attempts to make contact with her father (an overture her mother forbids) run throughout the memoir and provide a sort of controlling focus in her chaotic life; the memoir culminates in their reunion. In a 1975 interview, Mullen recalled that her father had gained some fame for his part in the production of Robert Flaherty's documentary *Man of Aran*.[5] When she arrived, he was engaged in writing an account of the film's production. Her father instructed her to write five hundred words of her own that he in turn sent on to Fabers, which commissioned the rest of the book.[6]

That book became *Life Is My Adventure*. Her father's literary instincts were good: the unusual story that Mullen had to tell was that of a young woman whose talents as an Irish step dancer led her into the unpredictable world of show business. Mullen opens her story in 1927, at an amateur competition in Topsfield, Massachusetts, and goes on to recall her abortive attempt to "make it," at age thirteen, as a dancer on the vaudeville stage and in the ethnic nightclubs. She was supervised in this attempt by an adult woman

3. *New Statesman and Nation*, June 26, 1937.
4. *New York Times*, October 24, 1937.
5. *Man of Aran*, directed by Robert Flaherty (1934).
6. "Return to Murder," *Guardian*, July 30, 1975. In this interview on the occasion of Mullen's return to the role of Miss Marple, Mullen states that both her father and brother were writing books. Her father's book was *Man of Aran* (New York: E. P. Dutton, 1935). He later wrote two accounts of life in the west of Ireland, *Hero Breed: A Novel* (New York: R. M. McBride, 1937) and *Come Another Day* (London: Faber and Faber, 1940). Her brother P.J. did not publish a book, but became a celebrated Aran Islander; his family ran a guest house at Kilronan on the main island until recent years.

accordionist, Katherine Leary, and by an assortment of older cousins and friends. Mullen's account of a life in Irish music is, in itself, a story of sufficient historical interest to warrant renewed attention in this work. Perhaps because of the innate informality of traditional music, the world of the Irish musician is one that has rarely been expressed in print; not until Terence Winch's poems in *Irish Musicians/American Friends* (1985)[7] or Ciaran Carson's autobiographical *Last Night's Fun* (1996)[8] have any writers succeeded as well as Mullen in evoking an Irish music subculture in a particular time and place. Moreover, Mullen's account is probably the only such account that unabashedly admits that folk music has a business side. Fintan Vallely, a prominent historian of Irish folk music, observes that the Irish traditional music community has long shunned the very thought of professionalism, preferring to believe that the music somehow perpetuated itself through love and mystical communion among players. The reality is, as Vallely writes, "that there had always been a commercial life, and that music in Ireland was no different than anywhere else [in that] it could provide both supplementary income and support full-time professionals."[9] Mullen in no way romanticizes the lives of professional entertainers.

After winning the New England Step Dancing championship, Mullen and her mother receive an unexpected call from Katherine Leary, a haughty woman who always appends the title "the world's champion accordion player" to her name. Leary first tries to buffalo Mullen's mother. "'My dear woman, your daughter has ability. Great ability. And I am the woman to give her her chance. Inside one year, I can make her as famous as I am myself,' she said slowly, impressively."[10] The truth, however, soon becomes clear: "the

7. Terence Winch, *Irish Musicians/American Friends* (Minneapolis: Coffee House Press, 1985).

8. Ciaran Carson, *Last Night's Fun: A Book about Traditional Irish Music* (New York: Macmillan, 1996).

9. Fintan Vallely, "The Making of a Lifelong *Companion*," *New Hibernia Review* 4, no. 2 (Summer 2000): 151.

10. Mullen, *Life*, 44.

Dancing Like Merry Hell

world's greatest accordion player" can barely make ends meet, but is convinced that—if she puts her two boys in a home, and if her alcoholic husband stays sober—she can make it big in New York. It is she who needs a step dancer to round out the act.[11]

From the start, Mullen and Leary's attempted entry into show business was impracticable, if not downright quixotic. In the late 1920s, vaudeville houses were rapidly disappearing under pressure from movies and radio. Almost the only option left to paid entertainers was to reinvent their acts for nightclubs.[12] Leary and Mullen's first paying job is not in a theater, but rather at McCluskey's Irish-American Hotel, Cabaret, and Restaurant at Rockaway—where, it turns out, Leary must also cook during the day while her daughter works as a waitress. McCluskey's proves a disaster. The proprietor is a raging alcoholic who turns their first night into a near riot. In New York, Leary and Mullen subsist on "[pan]cakes and water" and make a steady round of booking agents, occasionally landing a one-night engagement but usually hearing "come back next week."[13] They even broadcast Irish music from the World's Radio Fair at Madison Square Garden, where, in a farcical scene, Mullen is compelled to dance on a desktop for radio listeners. Her most visible public performance comes in an "Irish Fair" at Boston Garden, where she dances before a crowd estimated at 10,000. There, on the last night of the show, Barbara is saddened to learn in the dressing room that a nice young man from the Fahey Orchestra has been killed in a car accident and wonders if the act will still play. Another girl gives Mullen a blunt lesson when she tells her, "Of course the act went on. The crowd paid money to see the show, they want to get their money's worth. What do they care who dies or doesn't die?"—a lesson in show-business cynicism underscored when the promoter skips out without paying.[14]

11. Ibid., 48.
12. On the late days of vaudeville, see Edward B. Marks, *They All Sang: From Tony Pastor to Rudy Vallee*, as told to A. J. Liebling (New York: Viking Press, 1935).
13. Mullen, *Life*, 77.
14. Ibid., 172.

Yet, however seedy the realities of an entertainer's life may be, there are also passages in *Life Is My Adventure* that evoke the joyous character of Irish music and the expansive, welcoming environment in which it is played. A vigorous music scene grows up around Mullen and Leary in their pathetic New York apartment:

It was not unusual to see Maggie Murphy, Mr. Martin, Aunt B., Uncle Tom, and Mary sitting close together, side by side on the couch-bed, while Katherine, Mr. Gleason, Jimmy Hines, and Arthur Fucher (two young violinists) and several other musicians, sat on chairs or boxes in the middle of the kitchen floor, playing jigs and reels at top speed from eight o'clock till after midnight, stopping only at intervals to discuss the points of different tunes, or for tea and cakes at ten o'clock.[15]

Mullen says of her guardian's playing that "I have since heard better players, but none I have heard or will I ever hear who from her fingers could get the same heart, the same feeling, the same desire to dance into your feet, as Katherine Leary."[16] Describing the capacity of Irish music to bring her out of herself, Mullen says that "when I heard music I forgot everything else, and was happy, dancing as long as anyone would play for me. And so it was on this day [at the competition]. All my nervousness faded away, and I danced like merry hell."[17]

"When I heard music, I forgot everything else." There was, in fact, much in Mullen's life of urban poverty that she had good reason to want to forget. *Life Is My Adventure* is one of a number of Irish-American stories about missing out on the American Dream. In fiction, James T. Farrell's *Studs Lonigan* trilogy of the 1930s[18] and William Kennedy's Albany cycle, notably *Ironweed* (1983),[19] anchor the tradition. Among memoirists, the list would include *The Hard Road to Klondike* (originally written in Irish), in which Michael MacGowan

15. Ibid., 97. 16. Ibid., 44–45.

17. Ibid., 30.

18. James T. Farrell, *Young Lonigan* (New York: Vanguard, 1932); *The Young Manhood of Studs Lonigan* (New York: Vanguard, 1934); and *Judgment Day* (New York: Vanguard, 1935).

19. William Kennedy, *Ironweed* (New York: Viking, 1983).

is left behind to freeze to death on his way to the Alaska gold fields,[20] and Jim Tully's literal nostalgia for the gutter in *Beggars of Life* (1924)[21] and the autobiographical novel *Shanty Irish* (1928),[22] highlighting his ditch-digger grandfather. Mullen's book similarly belongs in this tradition of Irish-American shortfall, in part because it also opens a window on an enduring anomaly within the larger story of Irish-America's rise to affluence: South Boston.[23]

Boston, during the years of Mullen's childhood in the 1920s, remained the most ethnically riven, class-conscious city in the Northeast; throughout the economic boom of the decade, the city's unemployment often reached as high as 15 percent. Eighty years after waves of Famine-era immigrants had overwhelmed the city's genteel pretensions, many of the Irish had begun to make their move into middle-class respectability. But the neighborhood of Southie, where Mullen and her family lived, lagged behind both economically and culturally: the Irish subculture of Southie was in many ways an affront to Yankee propriety.[24] Mullen's family and friends take a casual attitude toward education; their Catholic religion appears only in its most cultic forms; and civil authority, in the form of the police and the courts, is an enemy to be avoided at all costs. Poverty and criminality force a hand-to-mouth improvisational lifestyle on the household; Mullen recalls that

20. Mící Mac Gabhann, *Rotha Mór an tSaoil* (Indreabhán, Conamara: Cló Iar-Chonnachta, 1997); the English version is Michael MacGowan, *The Hard Road to Klondike*, trans. Valentin Iremonger (London: Routledge and Kegan Paul, 1973).

21. Jim Tully, *Beggars of Life* (New York: Albert and Charles Boni, 1924).

22. Tully, *Shanty Irish* (New York: Albert and Charles Boni, 1928).

23. One cannot help but notice that "Ma," the heroine of Michael Patrick Mac-Donald's 1999 memoir of the 1970s South Boston busing crisis, *All Souls* (discussed in chap. 8), also finds herself scratching out a living as a part-time Irish musician—a full fifty years after Mullen's story.

24. See William V. Shannon, "Boston Irish," in *The American Irish* (New York: Macmillan, 1963), 182–200. For a discussion of South Boston's increasing separatism from the larger community in the 1920s, see James J. Connolly, *The Triumph of Ethnic Progressivism: Urban Political Culture in Boston, 1900–1925* (Cambridge, Mass.: Harvard University Press, 1998), esp. chap. 5, "James Michael Curley and the Politics of Ethnic Progressivism," 133–60.

[W]e had more customers than any other speakeasy in the district. There was plenty of money coming in. But as fast as we made it it was spent again, in paying fines whenever we were raided and the stuff was found, which was frequently . . . every time the bootlegger . . . was paid, it took all the ready cash that was in the house, and we had to depend on Saturday's business to get Sunday's dinner, or anything else.[25]

When Barbara slips on a ferryboat and injures her back a few days before a dance competition, her mother's instinct for survival comes to the fore. She advises her daughter to stay in bed: "You probably wouldn't win anyway. . . . We may get something out of the boat people if you stay in bed a while."[26]

After Mullen is arrested for selling bootleg whiskey to a police informant, a vigilante group in the neighborhood metes out street-corner justice to the tipster; later, when she finds herself in front a of a judge, the young Mullen risks being cited for contempt of court by shouting an obscenity at her accuser. The family moves incessantly, trains a vicious dog to look out for the cops, and keeps a bottle of disinfectant at the ready to pour into the bootlegged liquor to disqualify it as evidence. If Mullen and her mother had thought that going on the road in New York would put an end to such extemporization, they were wrong. In New York, paid work is so scarce that Leary and Mullen steal milk from their neighbors' doorsteps and order meals at restaurants and skip out on the tab. At public events, Mullen and the rest of Leary's entourage stuff her instrument case with cold cuts while no one is looking, and—in a scene that might have appeared in Laurel and Hardy—they pull "the midnight flit" on their rent by sneaking their trunks down the stairs while the landlady sleeps.

We can laugh at these incidents, and the title that Mullen chose for her memoir implies a brave face and a roll-with-the-punches attitude; but reading this book today it is difficult not to feel the

25. Mullen, *Life*, 23.
26. Ibid., 16.

sadness of a child caught up in this dysfunctional world. Writing of recent Irish autobiography, Jane Elizabeth Dougherty compares *Angela's Ashes* (1996) with Nuala O'Faolain's memoir *Are You Somebody* (1996) and notes that "If McCourt, in his memoirs, never stops being a child, then O'Faolain, in hers, never really is one." In O'Faolain's childhood—and, we shall see, in Mullen's—the girls are treated not as children but as little adults. Dougherty asks, "Where is the Irish girlhood?"[27] Wherever it is, or was, the Irish girlhood is seldom found in the record left by women memoirists. Here is Mullen's sobering opening paragraph:

I cannot remember a time when I did not want to run away from home. When I was very young I used to wonder if I could not find a band of gipsies who would take me along with them. Later, as I grew older, I got as far as packing a small bag and saving pennies. But gradually what courage I had was being beaten out of me. I learned that the easiest way was the best way to get along. My only comfort was my books. No one was interested enough to wonder what books I read.... I came to know of a world entirely different from that in which I lived. I learned of people who spoke nicely to each other, who had shelves of good books, and who believed in helping each other; of others that swore and drank and fought all day, and what decent people thought of them. Slowly I began to understand that I had been wrong to let my mother crush my beliefs and mould my character as she saw fit. "How can I be a person if I think only what I'm told to think and feel only what I'm told to feel?" I asked myself.[28]

Mullen, in fact, grows up in a household bereft of parental nurturance, where the father has fled to Ireland and the mother is too preoccupied buying and selling liquor to attend any of Mullen's dance performances. When her mother displays pride in her daughter's achievements, she does so in a perversely adult manner: after her

27. Jane Elizabeth Dougherty, "Are You Angela? Gendered Narratives of Irish Childhoods," conference presentation, American Conference For Irish Studies, Fordham University, June 2002; see also Dougherty, "Nuala O'Faolain and the Unwritten Irish Girlhood," *New Hibernia Review* 11, no. 2 (Summer 2007): 50–65.

28. Mullen, *Life*, 9–10.

daughter brings home a trophy cup, the mother fills it with whiskey and passes it around, allowing her customers to get roaring drunk on the house. Except for her antagonistic brother Puffy, the narrator moves in a world almost without children. At home in Boston, she falls asleep in school because of her exhausting schedule of dancing and teaching (all the money from which is turned over to her mother), and she makes no friends; the other girls mock her because of her mother's frequent arrests. After moving to New York in Leary's care, Barbara suggests that she should be starting school soon. She discovers that this is not going to be allowed. "She [Leary] put me on solid ground when she said: 'Oh you have had enough education. You must now think of your career as a dancer.'"[29] The thirteen-year-old Barbara's indenture to Katherine Leary is only possible if the young dancer lies about her age and takes to wearing cosmetics, and when, after a year of fruitless searching for stardom in New York, she is returned to Boston, Leary's kindly Aunt B. tells her, "We've done you a great deal of harm ... growing you up and making a woman of you when you were still a child.... We have taken your childhood away from you."[30]

Actually, her initiation into the world of adults began well before her time in New York: drunks, leering barflies, and police raids were part of the landscape of Mullen's childhood from an early age. The one area where Mullen is shielded from adult life is with regard to sex; her mother takes great care to be sure that Barbara remains in the dark about sex until late in the book, when an adult cousin prevails on some other girls to explain the facts of life. The older girls remark that in this instance Mullen seems "as if she'd been kept in a convent" since infancy.[31] Whether she is prematurely streetwise or unexpectedly naïve, the life that Mullen narrates in *Life Is My Adventure* proves to be another version of the girlhood that never was.

It is therefore not surprising that Mullen fantasizes about run-

29. Ibid., 81. 30. Ibid., 139.
31. Ibid., 266.

ning away or that her dreams of escape come to be fixated on her father across the sea in the primitive west of Ireland. The fact that Mullen is able, through intermediaries, to establish a correspondence with the father should not obscure the reality that he has effectively abandoned his family. In the mother-daughter relationship that Mullen is thus forced to negotiate on her own, her life in dance is only the most visible site of contention in what is at bottom a deeply conflicted relationship. Her mother occasionally boasts of her daughter's dancing, but when she does she also claims a sort of ownership in her success for having first taught her traditional jigs and reels. But Mullen's mother is hardly supportive: she slights her daughter continually, sends her off as a child into the mercenary world of show business, and undermines her achievement at every turn. When Mullen's father sends dance costumes from the Aran Islands, the mother's resentment is so intense that she cuts them to ribbons rather than have him in any way involved with her daughter's success.

Threatened by her daughter's idealization of the absent father, Mullen's mother seeks to crush her daughter's will. At one point she is overheard to say of Barbara, "She's too much like the Mullens with her books, and reading, and queer notions. But I'll knock it out of her."[32] As Barbara perceives, she has been denied any claim on a self of her own; rather, her good qualities are claimed by her mother and her supposed shortcomings assigned to her father. "When my mother was in a merry mood she would always say at the finish: 'It's from me she took that,' but when her back was troubling her and her temper and nerves on edge, she says instead, bitingly: 'Just like what her father would do.'"[33]

Further, the family interprets her dance talents in a manner that subverts even her achievements on stage—the only means by which she might be allowed recognition. They conceive of her dancing, not as a consequence of Barbara's exertions, but as a "gift" for which she can take no credit:

32. Ibid., 19.
33. Ibid., 229.

My mother did not believe that I should ever find a job, though I had often made more than $15 in one evening by dancing. For dancing was something I had always been able to do. It wasn't the result of any effort on my part, it was just something that I took for granted, because I could not remember a time when I had not been able to dance, and the whole family felt the same way about it.[34]

Thus, though her life in Irish dance may indeed create an artistic space where she can find refuge, every time Mullen dances she also necessarily recalls her mother's systematic quelling of her identity.

The deep story of *Life Is My Adventure* is not of Mullen's misadventures in show business, but the story of a young woman moving out from under an oppressive environment, a narrative that reaches a turning point on her sixteenth birthday. By working as a hotel switchboard operator, she has gotten a taste of normal life, and on that day Mullen announces that she intends to quit dancing. Her brother exclaims, "But if she doesn't dance she'll be just another straphanger for the rest of her life," adding, "She can't do anything right except dance."[35] The mother agrees, but surprisingly, allows her daughter her to make up her own mind for the first time in her life. The sixteen-year-old hastens to jettison her dance career: "I'd much rather be working, or larking . . . on my days off, than do anything else. I don't want to dance."[36] And though the mother professes that she will honor Barbara's decision, she soon sets up a classic double-bind after her daughter declines a performance that might have brought some money into the house: "'Well it's up to yourself, of course' she said. 'But I think you're being very selfish.'"[37]

Mullen's family situation, then, involves an unengaged father; a controlling mother; double binds, including pressure to look and act older than she is and simultaneous pressure to remain asexual; and a young woman who, desperate to assert a measure of autonomy, cuts herself off, first, from the recognition, satisfaction,

34. Ibid., 229.   35. Ibid., 248.
36. Ibid., 249.   37. Ibid., 254.

and artistic expression she knows in dance, and second, from the very real financial reward that dancing brings.[38] This cluster of behaviors bears an unsettling resemblance to the social and psychological factors in many women with anorexia. The closing chapter makes the connection explicit and does so in a way that confirms the contemporary understanding of anorexia as a form of protest against the circumscription of women's lives.

Mullen's refusal to dance is followed by two important occasions where she surrenders to her mother; first, when the mother forces her to break off a relationship with a boy who has taken a serious interest in her, and second, when Barbara hands over a £20 note her father had sent to pay her passage to Ireland. She writes,

the moment I handed over the money, I changed. Not outwardly, but inwardly I seemed to shrivel up. . . . All my hopes, all my dreams, since I could remember, had been centred on my Father and P.J., and theirs in me, and now I had deliberately turned my back on them and let them down.

The change was gradual but definite. At first I felt numb; I ate, but didn't know whether I was eating or not. Then food began to sicken me; I could not eat at all. My mother wore herself out in cooking the dishes I liked best to try and tempt my appetite. I would push them away and have nothing but coffee.[39]

Insomnia, night terrors, outbursts of screaming, and a dramatic weight loss—from 132 to 101 pounds over six weeks—ensue. Her tailspin is arrested only when the mother agrees to let her go to Ireland if she will resume eating. Mullen does; but, having surrendered the original £20 to her mother, her need to assert her own agency is so great that she will not take it back. Instead, she works twice as hard as before in order to earn every penny of her fare to the

38. According to inflation calculation tables based on the annual Consumer Price Index, the $15 that Mullen states she could make in one night in the early 1930s would be equivalent to more than $260 today; see, for instance, "Inflation Calculator," at *http://data.bls.gov/cgi-bin/cpicalc.pl.*

39. Mullen, *Life*, 307–8.

Aran Islands. Mullen describes the reunion with her father on Inis Mór in the language of rescue; in fact, he reenters her life by arriving on a galloping white horse. Her father seizes her in a bear-hug, and as the book closes, she exults that "my spirit soared sky high as I thought to myself: 'Well, for goodness sakes! I've struck oil at last.'"[40]

An overstatement? Almost certainly; but the bad dream was over. Mullen ends her memoir here; but in her acting career she lived out the autobiographical archetype of the circuitous journey, in which the narrator opens with an intense image or preoccupation, moves away from it, and then returns to that preoccupation with a different understanding. Mullen rediscovered her performing life, which, before she jettisoned it, had consumed her childhood. Unencumbered by the emotional tug-of-war with her mother, Mullen found that on Inis Mór, "her entertaining 'came to a new beginning' because she danced and sang for the Islanders every night."[41] Eventually she went to drama school in England, and—no doubt in part through her father's contacts with Robert Flaherty and her marriage to John Taylor, who had been his cameraman on *Man of Aran*—went on to celebrity.

But all of that remained in the future when Mullen closed her autobiography. Read today, *Life Is My Adventure* more than bears out the truism that an entertainer's life often conceals a deep sadness. Although a lively music scene is its backdrop, precious little frivolity comes across in her autobiography. Rather, we see in it the story

40. Ibid., 319. The exclamation that closes Mullen's book not only resonates with her own pursuit of the famously elusive jackpot of show-business success, but, oddly, also seems to suggest the plots of several of her notable films. Her breakthrough film, *Jeannie*, directed by Harold French (1943), concerns a young woman who unexpectedly comes into an inheritance; the comedy *Talk of a Million* with Jack Warner, directed by John Paddy Carstairs (1951) and later released in the United States under the title *You Can't Beat the Irish*, involves a family of Irish ne'er-do-wells who believe, erroneously, that they've struck it rich; and the plot of the gangster drama *It Takes a Thief*, directed by John Gilling (1960), with Jayne Mansfield, revolves around a search for a stolen cache of loot from a bank heist.

41. "Return to Murder," *Guardian*, July 30, 1975.

Dancing Like Merry Hell

of a young woman desperate to interpret her own experience; even in our memoir-conscious era, few twenty-three-year-olds feel compelled to write their life history. Barbara Mullen danced her way through a not-very-merry hell; and she found a happier world, one that she describes as "different entirely from that in which I lived," only when the dancing stopped.

3

Joseph Mitchell's Irish Imagination

In October of 1929, Joseph Mitchell, a young writer of Scottish and English descent, arrived in New York from North Carolina. The twenty-one-year-old Mitchell had been hired, sight unseen, for his first reporting job covering police affairs for the *World*. In the next decade, Mitchell moved on to reporter and feature writer positions at the *Herald Tribune* and, later, the *World-Telegram*. He joined the staff of the *New Yorker* in 1938 and remained there until his death in May 1996, where his extraordinary care in research and composition helped to cement that publication's reputation for literary reportage. Calvin Trillin once dedicated a book to him as "the *New Yorker* reporter who set the standard."[1]

Although he lived in a city in which the Irish had dominated

An earlier version of this chapter appeared in *New Perspectives on the Irish Diaspora*, ed. Charles Fanning (Carbondale: Southern Illinois University Press, 2000), and is reprinted with permission.

1. Calvin Trillin, dedication, in *Killings* (New York: Ticknor and Fields, 1984). Despite his high reputation, there is still relatively little scholarly study of Joseph Mitchell and his work. An essential critical biography is Thomas Kunkel, *Man in Profile: Joseph Mitchell of the New Yorker* (New York: Random House, 2015); see also James Rogers and Norman Sims, "Joseph Mitchell," in *American Literary Journalists, 1945–1995 Dictionary of Literary Biography*, ed. Arthur Kaul (Detroit: Gale Research, 1997), 185, 199–210.

politics, the public safety departments, the unions, and construction for half a century—a city in which the census taken a year after his arrival disclosed some 220,000 foreign-born Irish living in New York City, 97,000 of them in the borough of Manhattan alone[2]—Mitchell's journalism holds limited value as a documentary source on the Irish in New York City. Yet a close reading of this most perceptive of journalists reveals that the Irish are nonetheless present as one of the "figures in the carpet" beneath his writing and, in a larger sense, beneath the city that he came to love. This figure comes to the fore in two ways: first, as an emblem of resistance to change; and second, as a tradition that reveres and is nourished by the spoken word.

That Mitchell was drawn to the Irish there is no doubt. After Mitchell's death, Brendan Gill recalled that "Joe loved the Irish as a people, and he would sit talking by the hour to old tads at McSorley's."[3] He traveled to Ireland on several occasions and was an early and lifelong member of the James Joyce Society. In the introduction to *The Bottom of the Harbor* (1960), he identifies Irish literature as one of the great fascinations of his life.[4] He professed to have read *Finnegans Wake* "at least half a dozen times" and specifically cites Joyce as a major influence.[5] In his most autobiographical work, Mitchell recalled having, at the age of twenty-four, "come under the spell of Joyce's 'Ulysses'" and wanting to write a comparable book that was equally encyclopedic about New York.[6]

When we recognize Mitchell's affinity for the Irish, one of the questions that arises is why the group does not figure more promi-

2. Ronald Bayor and Timothy Meagher, eds., *The New York Irish* (Baltimore: Johns Hopkins University Press, 1996), 560.

3. David Remnick, "Postscript: Joseph Mitchell; Three Generations of *New Yorker* Writers Remember the City's Incomparable Chronicler," *New Yorker*, June 10, 1996.

4. Joseph Mitchell, *The Bottom of the Harbor* (New York: Modern Library, 1994), v.

5. Mitchell, *Up in the Old Hotel* (New York: Pantheon, 1992), xii. *Up in the Old Hotel* collects four previously published books: *McSorley's Wonderful Saloon* (New York: Duell, Sloan and Pearce, 1943); *Old Mr. Flood* (New York: Duell, Sloan and Pearce, 1948); *The Bottom of the Harbor* (New York: Little Brown, 1960), and *Joe Gould's Secret* (New York: Viking, 1965). With the exception of a few sentences from introductory material, all quotations in this chapter are taken from *Up in the Old Hotel*.

6. Mitchell, *Up in the Old Hotel*, 690.

nently in his reporting. Two reasons—one temperamental and one sociological—suggest themselves to explain the relative paucity of Irish references in Mitchell's attempt to chronicle New York. The temperamental one is that he was, at times, a writer with a gift for overlooking the large; one able to write a detailed portrait of New York's skid row in the 1930s without mentioning the Depression, and one able to omit all mention of World War II from his writing in the 1940s. The sociological explanation tells us more. Mitchell's arrival came at the very end of an era when, as one historian notes, "The Irish ruled New York. . . . They controlled its government and politics, dominated construction and building, moved into the professions and the managerial classes, and benefited, perhaps disproportionately, from the general prosperity of the times."[7] The creeping middle-class status of the Irish, their assimilation into conventional roles in society—public safety, education, and the professions—with an attendant draining of "color," probably kept Mitchell, with his innate taste for the offbeat, from paying more attention to them. The New York Irish were losing the distinctive characteristics that attracted Mitchell even as he was making them his own. Mitchell would have understood precisely what Lawrence McCaffrey meant when he said of a later generation's move to the suburbs that the Irish had moved "from somewhere to nowhere."[8]

Those Irish and Irish Americans who appear in Mitchell's journalism display many of the traits that Mitchell prized: a refusal to participate in commercial society, a heroic attempt to stay behind the times, a fear that the world passed on to future generations will no longer be, in one of his favorite words, "genuine." Thus, Mitchell's Irish perform a sort of literary ventriloquism; as they speak, they give voice to the author's own concerns and preoccupations.

At first blush, though, Joseph Mitchell's Irish appear to be not all that different from those presented by the image makers of

7. Chris McNickle, "When New York Was Irish, and After," in Bayor and Meagher, *New York Irish*, 337.
8. Lawrence J. McCaffrey, *The Irish Diaspora in America* (Bloomington: Indiana University Press, 1976), 152.

the tourist industry—as a people who love drink and sentimental songs. One of his early newspaper features profiled John Hassett, a singing plumber's helper from the Bronx. Hassett, though only twenty-five, refuses to expand his repertoire beyond the "old Irish favorites" he learned at the Shamrock Democratic Club. Hassett sings such chestnuts as "That's How I Spell Ireland" at the drop of a hat, anytime, anywhere; Mitchell meets him in the locker room of the Brooklyn Dodgers, where, despite being a no-field left-handed second baseman, he is getting a tryout because Casey Stengel likes to hear him sing "The Last Rose of Summer."[9] Music also appears in Mitchell's 1939 "Obituary of a Gin Mill," which laments the gentrification of Dick's Saloon, once beloved for its impromptu Friday "cabaret nights," when a "beery old saloon musician would show up with an accordion and a mob of maudlin rummies would surround him to sing hymns and Irish songs."[10]

Mitchell describes the all-male, Tammany-run fundraising events of pre-Prohibition days known as "Beefsteaks" in "All You Can Hold for Five Bucks." Here, one of the chefs recalls, "At the old beefsteaks they almost always had storytellers, men who would entertain with stories in Irish and German dialect. And when the people got tired of eating and drinking, they would harmonize. You could hear them harmonizing blocks away. They would harmonize 'My Wild Irish Rose' until they got their appetite back."[11] In "Mazie," a 1940 piece set in a Bowery movie house where bums sleep off hangovers and retreat from the street, readers encounter a down-and-out "courtly old Irishman named Pop" who spends his nights singing ballads in "Irish gin mills on Third Avenue"—including "Whiskey, You're the Divil," "The Garden Where the Praties Grow," "Tiddly-Aye-Aye for the One-Eyed Reilly," and "The Widow McGinnis's Pig."[12]

Clearly, the face that the Irish presented to Mitchell was often a face found in a barroom. As it happens, the *New Yorker*'s "Irish

---

9. Mitchell, *My Ears Are Bent* (New York: Sheridan House, 1938), 144.
10. Mitchell, *Up in the Old Hotel*, 246.   11. Ibid., 295.
12. Ibid., 33.

saloon beat," if we may call it that, was already being well covered by his colleague John McNulty, who made a specialty of chronicling Irish watering holes in Manhattan and collected some of his most popular fictionalized stories in *Third Avenue, New York* (1946).[13] Mc-Nulty's stories feature Runyonesque Irish characters with names like Grogan the Horseplayer, Paddy Ferrarty the Bartender, and Little Mike and Grady, two cabdrivers. Mitchell turned his journalistic attentions elsewhere, but the sorts of establishments that McNulty wrote about do appear in his work. For instance, Mitchell's fictional slice-of-life story "The Kind Old Blonde" opens in "Shine's, an Irish restaurant near the Pennsylvania Station."[14] The Native American bridge workers profiled in "The Mohawks in High Steel" hang out in Nevins Bar and Grill in Brooklyn, of which Mitchell admiringly notes, "The Nevins is small and snug and plain and old. It is one of the oldest saloons in Brooklyn. It was opened in 1888, when North Gowanus was an Irishtown, and it was originally called Connelly's Abbey. Irish customers still call it the Abbey."[15] Elsewhere he mentions a Bowery saloon called John McGurk's Suicide Hall.[16] He meets the Don't-Swear Man, a colorful anti-profanity crusader, when, as he relates, "One dank afternoon I dropped into Shannon's, an Irish saloon on the southeast corner of Third Avenue and Seventy-sixth Street, and ordered a split of Guinness."[17]

McNulty's and Mitchell's Irish differ in their degrees of participation. The Irish characters in McNulty's vignettes draw their energy from the hustle and vitality of urban life and, in turn, create part of the colorful ambiance that was New York in the 1930s. In contrast, Mitchell's Irish—like so many of the figures who inhabit Mitchell's New York—step away from the modern world and turn their gaze back to better days behind.

13. John McNulty, *Third Avenue, New York* (Boston: Little, Brown, 1946). Other books by McNulty are *A Man Gets Around* (Boston, Little Brown, 1951); *The World of John McNulty* (New York: Doubleday, 1957); and the posthumously collected *This Place on Third Avenue* (Washington, D.C., Counterpoint, 2001).

14. Mitchell, *Up in the Old Hotel*, 337.　　15. Ibid., 285.
16. Ibid., 130.　　17. Ibid., 232.

Joseph Mitchell's Irish Imagination

Mitchell wrote almost nothing about electoral politics. His 1938 anthology of newspaper features, *My Ears Are Bent*, however, contains a section called "Our Leaders" in which several stingingly ironic portraits of political hacks appear. One memorable Irish American, Peter J. McGuinness, a stevedore-turned-politician from the neighborhood of Greenpoint (famed as the birthplace of Brooklynese), provides the subject of one of these profiles, "Mr. McGuinness Puts a Stop to the Machine Age." Mitchell wrote:

I like Mr. Peter J. McGuinness because he is hearty and outspoken, because he is one of the last of the old-time neighborhood statesmen, and because he will give an interview on any subject under the sun, no matter how abstruse, without a bit of hesitation. Mr. McGuinness once characterized himself as "the Fighting Alderman from Greenpoint, the Garden Spot of the World," and he prides himself on his incessant warfare against women cigaret smokers, Chinese coolies, cabaret cover charges and the abolition of the Greenpoint ferry.[18]

An honest politician, McGuinness was nonetheless what newspaper people call "good copy"; the aside about women cigarette smokers refers to a farcical incident in which New York cops thought that the legislation McGuinness had introduced had already passed and went out rounding up women who smoked in public. Mitchell recalls an interview with McGuinness on the subject of technocracy. The alderman lacks a sophisticated vocabulary of social analysis, but he knows very well what changing technology means for the people in his district:

I told him [McGuinness] I wanted an interview on technocracy, and he said, "What is it?" I began a rough explanation, which he soon interrupted. He said that he was one of the original prophets of technocracy and that the 1928 minutes of the Greenpoint Peoples' Regular Democratic Club would prove it.

"I seen it coming," he said. "Away back in 1928 I seen the machine age coming. One night at a meeting in the clubhouse I warned my constituents against the machine age. Technocracy is nothing new to

18. Mitchell, *My Ears Are Bent*, 263.

me. As far back as 1928 I seen it coming. So far as I know I was one of the first to speak about it."[19]

McGuinness rants on about how draymen are being thrown out of work by trucks and how a pretzel factory in his district has laid off twenty women due to automation. Mitchell continues,

The former alderman looked at his desk. The sight of his dial telephone made him angry. "And look at this," he said, "it's got so everything is hooked up to a machine." I asked him if he had thought of a way to put a stop to the machine age.

"I have," he said. "Every machine the patent office down at Washington puts their O.K. on will do away with the work of men. There ought to be a stop put to the work done by the patent office. Just notify them they can't O.K. any more of these machines. We got to put a stop to the machine age, and so far as I know that's the best way."[20]

There is mockery here, yes—but there is also affection. Mitchell respects his subject's aggressive naïveté. McGuinness's suggestion that the patent office simply call a halt to the machine age is, of course, preposterous, and Mitchell delights in the outrageousness of the idea. At the same time, Mitchell also understands that as times progress, decent men and women are losing familiar and cherished parts of their world. Mitchell's journalism often celebrates retreat: working men withdrawing to their taverns, the young man who sings only the old Irish standbys, McGuinness fuming against technology, and the majestic anachronism so warmly evoked in Mitchell's 1940 piece "The Old House at Home," first collected in his 1943 volume *McSorley's Wonderful Saloon*.

McSorley's, just off Cooper Square in Greenwich Village, was then (and remains still) the oldest bar in New York City. In many ways, it serves as the prototypical Irish bar in the United States. Harrigan and Hart's musical comedy "McSorley's Inflation" (1882) is set there. The bar's importance to the Irish community was examined in a 1987 documentary, scripted by Peter Quinn, which

19. Ibid., 264–65.
20. Ibid., 265–66.

shows how—despite having been opened to women, turned into a tourist mecca, and subjected to standing-room-only crowds of young people every night—McSorley's still trades on a reputation for changelessness.[21]

At the time of Mitchell's story, the bar was eighty-eight years old, and in that span had known only four owners, "an Irish immigrant, his son, a retired policeman, and his daughter—and all of them have been opposed to change."[22] It would no doubt please McGuinness that, when Mitchell reported on McSorley's, the owner still refused to answer the telephone he had grudgingly installed in 1925. The bar that Mitchell cherished was at best a reluctant participant in modern commercial society or, indeed, in modern time at all: "There is no cash register. Coins are dropped in soup bowls—one for nickels, one for dimes, one for quarters, and one for halves—and bills are kept in a rosewood cashbox. It is a drowsy place; the bartenders never make a needless move, the customers nurse their mugs of ale, and the three clocks on the walls have not been in agreement for many years."[23]

In Mitchell's time, McSorley's was patronized by "a rapidly thinning group of crusty old men, predominantly Irish, who have been drinking there since they were youths and now have a proprietary feeling about the place."[24] The saloon that Mitchell loved was founded on the backward look. John McSorley, Mitchell tells us, "patterned his saloon after a public house he had known in his hometown in Ireland—Omagh, in County Tyrone—and originally called it the Old House at Home."[25] Mitchell catalogs the oddments hung reverentially on the walls of McSorley's. They include such Irish-American tokens as shillelaghs, prints of Irish prizefighters, and an engraving of the "Rescue of Colonel Thomas J. Kelly and Captain Timothy Deacy by Members of the Irish Revolutionary Brotherhood from the English Government at Manchester, England, September 18, 1867"[26]—an

21. *McSorley's New York*, directed by Marcia Rock (1987).
22. Mitchell, *Up in the Old Hotel*, 3.   23. Ibid., 3.
24. Ibid., 3.   25. Ibid., 4.
26. Ibid., 7.

original from the days when New York's Fenians caballed in the dim corners of McSorley's. (Today, a framed chip of stone hangs behind the bar over a plaque that reads, "This immortal specimen was presented to McSorley's by Joseph Mitchell and Brendan Gill." The stone is in fact a fragment from Nelson's Pillar in Dublin, which was blown up by the IRA in 1966.)

The Irish Americans to whom McSorley handed on his tavern were resolute in their unwillingness to change. In his later years, Mitchell would devote much of his energy to such causes as historic preservation and reforestation; it is not surprising that he would admire the sense of custodianship with which the founder's son Bill ran the bar. He writes,

Throughout his life Bill's principal concern was to keep McSorley's exactly as it had been in his father's time. When anything had to be changed or repaired, it appeared to pain him physically. For twenty years the bar had a deepening sag. A carpenter warned him repeatedly that it was about to collapse; finally, in 1933, he told the carpenter to go ahead and prop it up. While the work was in progress he sat at a table in the back room with his head in his hands and got so upset he could not eat for several days.[27]

"The Old House at Home" concludes with a scene of the bartender Kelly nudging the old men who fall asleep in the afternoon sunlight of the wonderful saloon. Mitchell understands their rootedness in the familiar as a warm and humane blessing:

Kelly makes jokes about the constancy of the old men. "Hey, Eddie," he said one morning, "old man Ryan must be dead!" "Why?" Mullins asked. "Well," Kelly said, "he ain't been in all week." In summer they sit in the back room, which is as cool as a cellar. In winter they grab the chairs nearest the stove and sit in them, as motionless as barnacles, until around six, when they yawn, stretch, and start for home, insulated with ale against the dreadful loneliness of the old and alone. "God be wit' yez," Kelly says as they go out the door.[28]

27. Ibid., 8–9.
28. Ibid., 22.

Joseph Mitchell's Irish Imagination

Like McSorley's, Mitchell himself elected not to be mastered by any clocks or deadlines. Virtually his entire output for the 1950s is found in one collection of six stories, *The Bottom of the Harbor*. In 1965 he published the enigmatic *Joe Gould's Secret*,[29] a book-length follow-up on a piece he had written twenty-three years earlier. After it appeared, Mitchell continued to go in to work at the *New Yorker*. However, until his death nearly thirty-two years later, he never again submitted a single word for publication to the magazine.

If a journalist believes that the old ways are the best and that the contemporary world is less satisfying, less genuine, and less interesting than that which went before, then those convictions will shape the way in which he practices his trade. A corollary that follows from these convictions is that when a reporter tells a story, it is always derivative and by definition cannot hope to be as rich and full as is the original. In Mitchell's case, it seems clear that the original sources are informed by a particularly Irish privileging of orality. Noel Perrin has called attention to the "enormous courtesy" that pervades Mitchell's writing, a courtesy that translates into an innate respect for the role of the storyteller: "The ultimate courtesy is to accept people on their own terms—and more than accept them . . . to take them seriously, see them as they are or believe they are, and to value what you see."[30] When Mitchell wanted to learn about, for example, circus freaks or faith healers, he went to his subjects and let them speak for themselves.

And so, when Mitchell grew interested in gypsy fortune-telling, he opened a window on that world for his readers by letting them sit in on a lengthy disquisition by Captain Daniel Campion, the New York Police Department's expert on gypsies. Campion, a native of the Hell's Kitchen neighborhood, is "blue-eyed and black-haired, and he has a calm, ruddy, observant, handsome, strong-jawed, Irish face."[31] The account is given almost completely in a monologue by

29. Mitchell, *Joe Gould's Secret*.

30. Noel Perrin, "Paragon of Reporters: Joseph Mitchell," *Sewanee Review* 91, no. 2 (Spring 1983): 169.

31. Mitchell, *Up in the Old Hotel*, 175.

Joseph Mitchell's Irish Imagination

Campion as he instructs two young detectives. Although Campion alludes to written files that he maintains on gypsies, they are patchy and secondary; the world of the gypsies has come to Campion and now to us almost entirely through oral sources.

In the same manner, Mitchell created an exhaustive and factually detailed portrait of the Fulton Fish Market in his 1948 book *Old Mr. Flood*. In the three long chapters of this book, a ninety-three-year-old "tough Scotch-Irishman" named Hugh G. Flood hands on the lore and the poetic language and traditions of the fishing industry in New York in story after story. Mitchell was in fact testing the boundaries between fiction and journalism—or to put it another way, he was carrying his practice of literary ventriloquism to an extreme level. Old Mr. Flood was an invented, composite character—fictitious, but, the author asserted, "solidly based on facts."[32] The merits of such a journalistic strategy can be debated, but the relevant point here is Mitchell's sense of history. When challenged to introduce an unfamiliar subculture to his readers, Mitchell instinctively relied on spoken tradition: go to an old man and tell the stories that he tells you.

This heightened respect for storytelling came early to Mitchell, while growing up in the rural South, and it was a tradition that as an adult he found resonant in Irish life and literature. Most of Mitchell's brief introduction to his omnibus collection *Up in the Old Hotel* (1992) is given over to recalling how childhood in an oral culture influenced his "cast of mind"—a childhood in which, after picnics, his aunts Mary and Annie would lead a procession out to the family graveyard at Iona Presbyterian Church. He writes of his aunt that she "wore old-fashioned clothes and she often talked about 'the old times,' and we thought of her as our link to the past."[33] The family progresses from grave to grave, each grave accompanied by a story.

32. Ibid., 373. Kunkel's 2015 biography created great controversy among Mitchell aficionados by revealing that some of Mitchell's journalistic practice was less "solidly based on facts" than has been assumed.
33. Mitchell, *Up in the Old Hotel*, xi.

Joseph Mitchell's Irish Imagination

"This man buried here," she would say, "was a cousin of ours, and he was so *mean* I don't know how his family stood him. And this man here," she would continue, moving along a few steps, "was so *good* I don't know how his family stood him." And then she would become more specific. Some of the things she told us were horrifying and some were horrifyingly funny.

I am an obsessive reader of *Finnegans Wake*—I must've read it at least half a dozen times—and every time I read the Anna Livia Plurabelle section I hear the voices of my mother and my aunts as they walk among the graves in old Iona cemetery and it is getting dark.[34]

An Irish preoccupation with listening lies at the heart of Mitchell's last book, *Joe Gould's Secret*. Mitchell devoted six years of his career to writing this memoir of a Greenwich Village bohemian. Originally the subject of a 1942 Mitchell profile, Joe Gould is a Harvard-educated misfit who has lived on the streets of New York for decades. Among other foibles, he claims to be able to converse with seagulls and to have translated Longfellow into the seagulls' language. For decades, Gould has supposedly devoted his life to gathering materials for an enormous collection of transcribed conversations called the "Oral History of Our Times"—the first usage of the term "oral history," incidentally. No one has ever seen the "Oral History," but by its compiler's count it consists of some nine million words. *Joe Gould's Secret* chronicles Mitchell's relationship with Gould and his mighty work-in-progress over more than two decades. Mitchell balances pity, annoyance, and respect for Gould until, at a certain point, we realize that Gould's vast project of collecting the speech of daily life parallels the author's own project of journalism. In some funhouse-mirror sort of way, the derelict Gould overlaps with Mitchell himself. Like Mitchell, Gould began his time in New York as an aspiring reporter. He tells Mitchell of the moment when the idea for the Oral History came to him:

One morning in the summer of 1917, I was sitting in the sun on the back steps of [police] Headquarters recovering from a hangover.

34. Ibid., xii.

Joseph Mitchell's Irish Imagination

In a second-hand bookstore, I had recently come across and looked through a little book of stories by William Carleton, the great Irish peasant writer, that was published in London in the eighties and had an introduction by William Butler Yeats, and a sentence in Yeats's introduction had stuck in my mind: "The history of a nation is not in parliaments and battlefields, but in what the people say to each other on fair days and high days, and in how they farm, and quarrel, and go on pilgrimage." All at once, the idea for the Oral History occurred to me: I would spend the rest of my life going about the city listening to people—eavesdropping, if necessary—and writing down whatever I heard them say that sounded revealing to me, no matter how boring or idiotic or vulgar or obscene it might sound to others.[35]

Mitchell's writing abounds with genealogies—something of an Irish quality itself—and in this case, we can trace a line of descent that runs back from Mitchell, who began as a reporter, to Gould, who began as a newsboy, to the nineteenth-century novelist William Carleton, who first wrote for the *Christian Examiner*, and from there back to shanachies and storytellers of earlier ages—of whom, it would seem, journalists are merely the culturally impoverished heirs.

Mitchell's masterpiece, *The Bottom of the Harbor*, is suffused with the sense that the world is getting worse, and in aesthetic protest he portrays men who struggle to preserve a vanishing way of life—such as the shad fishermen of Edgewater, New Jersey, who, across the river from the Manhattan skyline, still hand-set their nets as they have done for centuries; the fishing captain who "once threatened to fire a man in his crew because he worked too hard";[36] and the old African American tending a graveyard on Staten Island.

The general trajectory of Mitchell's career traces a movement from the eccentric to the elegiac, and in tracking the Irish figures sprinkled throughout his journalism we find the same pattern. The Irish New Yorkers in the early work of Joseph Mitchell—who exalt personality above success and refuse to go along with the times—prefigure Mitchell's great later themes. The old pensioners

35. Ibid., 644.
36. Ibid., 544.

warming themselves by the stove in McSorley's introduce the deepest concern of Mitchell's mature work, his profound sense of mortality.

Joseph Mitchell's Irish form part of a project of bricolage—found objects pieced into an overarching story to present New York to the world. Mitchell constructed the Irish in a way that was informed by his deepest preoccupations. If we look closely, we find that Mitchell then took that construction and turned it around: in his taste for the eccentric, in his writings about those on the margins of society, in his admiration for those who resisted the increasing commercialism of the times, and in his celebration of oral tradition he went on to construct New York in Irish ways. If, from this, we can infer that there is an identifiably Irish way to practice the craft of reporting, then looking further along these lines might tell us something new about the Irish experience. For one thing, such an inquiry might suggest reasons so many talented Irish Americans chose journalism as a profession.

4

The Honeymooners

Jackie Gleason's Memoir of Brooklyn

Two of the most successful television series in history involve an ensemble cast of four and take place chiefly in a New York City apartment. One is *Seinfeld*, 1989–98, which had been initially dismissed as "too Jewish" and "too New York."[1] The other is *The Honeymooners*, 1955–56, which follows the lives of bus driver Ralph Kramden and sewer worker Ed Norton, as well as their much put-upon wives, Alice and Trixie, in the Bensonhurst neighborhood of Brooklyn. The show could hardly be more "New York" (the cast leaves the city in just one episode), but it is rarely understood as portraying any particular ethnic group. In theory, the series had been carefully stripped of any ethnic signifiers.

Indeed, *The Honeymooners* appeared precisely as American television underwent a sudden and dramatic process of "de-ethnicization." In *Time Passages: Collective Memory and American Popular Culture*, George Lipsitz observes that quite discernibly around 1954, television

---

1. See Steven Battaglia, "The Biz: The Research Memo that Almost Killed *Seinfeld*," *TV Guide*, June 27, 2014, http://www.tvguide.com/news/seinfeld-research-memo-1083639/.

ethnics started to disappear from the screen. Early shows had presented such groups and individual characters as Jews in *The Goldbergs* (1949–57), Italians in *Life With Luigi* (1952), blacks in *Amos 'n Andy* (1951–53), Scots in *Hey, Jeannie* (1956–57), Irish Americans to some extent in *The Life of Riley* (1949–50), in which Jackie Gleason had the original lead as a character who in some ways resembled *The Honeymooners'* Ralph Kramden, and the Norwegian immigrant family of *I Remember Mama* (1949). Abruptly, in the middle of the first Eisenhower administration, such characters fell out of favor. Or, to be more accurate, television began to restrict its ethnic markings to those of the supposedly normative WASP. The airwaves stayed homogenized until the 1970s; one example would be Carl Reiner's rejected sitcom proposal in the 1960s about an unmistakably Jewish comedy writer named Buddy Sorrel, who in the end emerged on the *Dick Van Dyke Show*, second fiddle to the ultra-whitebread Rob and Laura Petrie of suburban New Rochelle.[2]

If we take time to look, though, we find Irish subtexts at play in the televised lives of Ralph and Alice Kramden. It may be true, as numerous recent commentators on the Irish in popular cultural have proposed, that in such a context Irishness functioned as a "safe" or "off-white" ethnicity.[3] A simpler explanation, though, would be that the quiet Irishness of the series originates with the life and origins of its creator, Jackie Gleason. Like all good writing, the comedy of *The Honeymooners* finds its roots in autobiography; Gleason employed a team of well-compensated writers, but his control of the scripts was absolute (and his personal improvisations were legendary).

Of course, the show has other sources. On one occasion Gleason said he was thinking of the George Kelly play *The Show-Off* when

2. George Lipsitz, *Time Passages: Collective Memory and American Popular Culture* (Minneapolis: University of Minnesota Press, 1990), chap. 3, "The Meaning of Memory: Family, Class, and Ethnicity in Early Network Television," 39–75.

3. See Diane Negra, ed., *The Irish in Us: Irishness, Performativity, and Popular Culture* (Durham: Duke University Press, 2006) for a forceful assertion that Irish-American identity is imbricated with whiteness and often tinged with racism.

he created the character of Ralph.[4] Other scholars point to a Laurel and Hardy vaudeville routine called "Friendly Neighbors," as well as a Don Ameche radio series of the postwar years, "The Bickersons," about a couple who quarreled nonstop.[5]

Nonetheless, when Gleason sketched out the world of the four working-class New Yorkers of the show, he drew heavily on his own childhood in Brooklyn.[6] The names of Irish New Yorkers populate the show. Neighbor kids are Judy Connor and Tommy Doyle, and other neighbors are Mrs. Fogarty, Mrs. Hannon, Mr. Riley, the Geraghtys, and the Grogans. The cop on the corner is also named Grogan (which seems to be a stereotypically New York Irish name, also found in the recurring characters of Grogan the Horseplayer in John McNulty's *This Place on Third Avenue* and in Damon Runyon's character, the tenderhearted gangster Aloysius "Butch" Grogan).[7] Ralph and Norton's coworkers and fellow lodge members at the Royal Order of Raccoons include Joes Cassidy, Frank McGillicuddy, Jerry Shaw, and Frank Haggerty—all the names of people with whom Gleason grew up. The autobiographical element in *The Honeymoon-*

4. There are times when Irish America seems as intricately intertwined as the Bloomsbury Group; George Kelly (1887–1974) was a minor playwright whose niece was the famous Grace Kelly of Philadelphia, later Princess Grace of Monaco.

5. Virginia Wright Wexman, "Returning from the Moon: Jackie Gleason and the Carnivalesque," in *Critiquing the Sitcom: A Reader*, ed. Joanne Morreale (Syracuse: Syracuse University Press, 2013), 296n13.

6. Much of the discussion here draws on the three very capable full-length biographies of Gleason. These are Jim Bishop, *The Golden Ham: A Candid Biography of Jackie Gleason* (New York: Simon and Schuster, 1956) a conventional celebrity biography, with a "warts and all" agenda that offended Gleason deeply; W. J. Weatherby, *Jackie Gleason: An Intimate Portrait of the Great One* (New York: Pharos Books, 1992), which takes a psychological approach to Gleason's life; and William A Henry II, *The Great One: The Life and Legend of Jackie Gleason* (New York: Doubleday, 1992), a very solid study that situates Gleason in the history of entertainment and popular culture. Extensive recollections of Gleason can be found in many memoirs by his contemporaries, such as Audrey Meadows, *Love, Alice: My Life as a Honeymooner* (New York: Crown, 1994), which is highly laudatory, and Steve Allen, *The Funny Men* (New York: Simon and Schuster, 1956), 145–63.

7. John McNulty, *This Place on Third Avenue* (Washington, D.C.: Counterpoint, 2001).

ers is on full display in the address of the Kramden's Bensonhurst apartment at 358 Chauncey Street, which was Gleason's address as a child. (Though Chauncey Street is actually in the Bushwick neighborhood; Gleason thought Bensonhurst sounded more "Brooklynesque.")

This is in no way to suggest that the autobiographical or Irish dimension is some sort of Rosetta Stone that can explain the show. Not at all. *The Honeymooners* can be appreciated and studied on dozens of levels that have nothing to do with Ireland or Irish America; none is more important than the fact it is often brilliant comedy. Within American popular culture, the show can also be located in the genealogy of comedy. It is striking how Gleason and Carney reprise fat Oliver and skinny Stan from Laurel and Hardy, and the series is known to be a source for the *Flintstones*, which debuted in 1960; Hanna-Barbera, the cartoon's creators, admitted the connection, and Gleason actually considered an infringement suit, which he later dropped after being persuaded that he did not want to be recalled as "the man who killed Fred Flintstone."[8] Noteworthy, too, is *The Honeymooners'* centrality to the endless train of sitcoms involving a buffoon husband and a level-headed wife.

The full story of *The Honeymooners* involves a complicated and anomalous broadcast history that runs from 1950 through 1970, starting with skits on Gleason's *Cavalcade of Stars* on the Dumont Network and continuing with periodic reunion episodes on the subsequent *Jackie Gleason Show.* Its place in popular culture rests on thirty-nine episodes (known to its many fans as the Classic 39), filmed twice weekly before a live audience. The shows ran from October 1955 through September 1956, a span of only thirteen months. These episodes have stayed in syndication literally for decades.

But certainly—or "soytanly," as the two Brooklyn residents who are its central characters would say—Gleason and the writers took care to present their characters as Everyman and to strip the show of any overt markers of nationality. Gleason himself said that there

8. "The Flintstones," http://www.imdb.com/title/tt0053502/trivia.

were "hundreds of Kramdens" in Brooklyn growing up—meaning the type, not the names; his co-star Audrey Meadows's memoir of the show notes that it deliberately chose a name that had no special ethnic identification. Gleason took pride in never having heard from anyone who was actually named Ralph Kramden. Ed Norton, too, is a consciously "neutral" name, if a bit more common; the character sometimes uses the middle initial L., which stands for (and this is almost too good to be true) "Lilywhite."

Those attempts at homogenizing the show failed. The creators may have tried to mask it, but Lipsitz himself, in the course of commenting on the blanching of the airwaves, states that Kramden and Norton are members of the "Irish working class."[9] *The Honeymooners* is shot through with second-order signifiers of its creator's Irish background.

Gleason was not just Irish; he was Brooklyn Irish, from the most ethnically conscious area of the nation's most ethnically diverse city. Norman Podhoretz, in recalling Brooklyn of the 1940s, wrote that "there were no Americans. . . . There were Jews and Negroes and Italians and Poles and Irishmen. Americans lived in New England, in the South, in the Midwest: alien people in alien places."[10]

The most obvious way in which *The Honeymooners* telegraphed its Irish dimensions was the simple fact that its leads were Jackie Gleason and Art Carney. One of Alice McDermott's fictional characters remarks that there are only eight Irish faces, and Gleason and Carney had two of them; a famous image of Gleason and Brendan Behan posing face-to-face has the symmetry of a Rorschach blot. Gleason and Carney were born a few months apart in 1918, to Irish Catholic parents. Jackie, the son of Herbert and Mae Kelly Gleason (his mother was Irish-born) had an early life that well demonstrates the axiom that comedians often come from sad homes. His only sibling, a sickly older brother named Clemence, died as a

9. Lipsitz, *Time Passages*, 40.
10. Quoted in Matthew Frye Jacobson, *Roots Too: White Ethnic Revival in Post–Civil Rights America* (Cambridge, Mass.: Harvard University Press, 2009), 190–91.

child. His father abandoned the family when Jackie was in grade school, and Gleason's teen years were spent fending for himself as his mother slipped further into depression and alcoholism. In Gleason's words, "she slaved away in Brooklyn flats as grim as the one in 'The Honeymooners' and . . . died when she was forty-nine."[11]

Art Carney, the son of Edward and Helen Farrell Carney, was born a few miles away in Yonkers and raised in comparative comfort in Mount Vernon, in suburban Westchester County.[12] He also looked Irish; in 1960, when there was talk of making a movie based on the life of the Catholic humanitarian Dr. Tom Dooley, Carney's Irish looks made him a strong contender for the title role (it should be noted that Carney and Gleason were also gifted actors when cast in non-comic roles). In 1957, Carney played the lead in a *Playhouse 90* drama, "The Fabulous Irishman," based on the life of Robert Briscoe, the lord mayor of Dublin, and his Irishness became more important to his persona as he grew older. In 1976, he starred in the dramatic series *Lanigan's Rabbi*, about an Irish-American cop and his friend, a rabbi, who investigate cold cases together; he narrated a 1981 children's story, "The Leprechaun's Christmas Gold," in an Irish brogue; and he had a part in a 1980s sitcom *The Cavanaughs* (1985–88), a sort of *All in the Family* knock-off set in South Boston.

But to understand *The Honeymooners* as an artifact of Irish America we need to look beyond the faces and names. A deeper sensibility runs through Jackie Gleason's masterpiece, a sensibility informed by Irish-American history. The show and its contexts exemplify what Daniel Tobin has usefully called an "Invisible Irishness."[13]

For instance, *The Honeymooners* employs space in a way that comes out of a particular history. Live television in the early days did not allow extravagant sets, but even so, the Kramden household strikes us as exceptionally claustrophobic. One suspects that

11. Weatherby, *Jackie Gleason*, 9–10.

12. Michael Seth Starr, *Art Carney: A Biography* (New York: Fromm, 1997) is thus far the only full-length biography of the actor.

13. See Daniel Tobin, *Awake in America: On Irish American Poetry* (Notre Dame: Notre Dame University Press, 2011), 79.

this might be the real meaning of the lead character's name: they are, quite literally, "crammed in." Their home is a walk-up, with a fire escape out the window. It closely replicates the Gleason apartment on Chauncey Street. "There were never any curtains or draperies on the windows, no shades, because this is the way Jackie lived when he was young," according to the set decorator for *The Honeymooners*, who added that "Anything you see on the set is very definitely the way Jackie lived."[14] When set dressers hung a framed picture on the wall, he insisted it be taken down because his apartment had never had one. And in that enclosed space, much confirms the Yeatsian formula, "Out of Ireland have we come. / Great hatred, little room, Maimed us at the start."[15] Little room, to be sure: Alice and Trixie's homemaker lives are more confined than those of their husbands, but even when at work, the men are confined to the restricted spaces of bus routes and sewers.

Fractiousness is inevitable when people must rub shoulders with one another in such close quarters. In *Talking to the Dead*, Patrick Sheeran and Nina Witoszek make a strong case for identifying what they call "the querulous dyad" as a central trope of modern Irish writing and note the durability in Irish writing of paired cantankerous characters: "Irish dramaturgy abounds in querulous dyads. Lady Gregory's McInerney and Michael (*The Workhouse*), Synge's Old Mahon and Christy, O'Casey's Jockser and the Captain, Yeats Blind Man and Fool, Behan's Meg and Patrick, Murphy's James and Rosie, Beckett's Didi and Gogo, Lucky and Pozzo, Ham and Clove—all base their relationship on mutual antipathy based on verbal abuse."[16]

The two central relationships of Ralph and his maddening friend

14. Set decorator Pat Cuoco, quoted in Peter Crescenti and Bob Columbe, *The Official Honeymooners Treasury* (New York: Galahad, 1989), 208.

15. William Butler Yeats, "Remorse for Intemperate Speech," in *Selected Poems and Four Plays of William Butler Yeats*, ed. M. L. Rosenthal (New York: Scribner, 1996), 144.

16. Nina Witoszek and Patrick F. Sheeran, *Talking to the Dead: A Study of Irish Funerary Traditions* (Amsterdam: Rodopi, 1998), 157.

The Honeymooners

Norton and Ralph and his indispensable but sharp-tongued wife Alice exemplify this archetypal Irish tradition of querulous dyads. This is much truer of the early episodes than of the later. Those who viewed the forerunner episodes that were shown on the Dumont Network, when Alice was played by Pert Kelton, were often startled by the harshness of the earlier show. In the original sketches, Gleason is a young fat man married to a middle-aged battle-ax. Gleason's original suggestion for the series' title was, in fact, "The Beast." Over the course of the Classic 39, the show grows less bad-tempered (there seems to be no doubt that the characters were softened for the sake of the audience) but it is far from amicable. One of the certainties of *The Honeymooners* is that Ralph will lose his temper and berate those closest to him, though by the end of any episode, Ralph's antagonism will usually be tempered when he realizes he should grateful to the other: "Baby, you're the greatest," "Norton, you're a pal." No blow is ever struck, but the threat of physical violence appears in virtually every episode, and the verbal violence is continual. The definitive line of the series is Ralph, with a raised fist, warning his wife, "One of these days Alice. . . . To the moon!"

Locating *The Honeymooners* in time is a challenge. The show's internal chronology is inconsistent; scripts indicate that the couple have been married variously for fourteen or fifteen years, which would place their weddings right around the start of the Second World War, though in the Classic 39 episodes there is just one reference to the war (Norton mentions having been in the navy). There are also periodic suggestions that the couples are much older. At one point, Ralph mentions having practiced dancing the Charleston, an anachronism of more than twenty years. Both male leads were in their late thirties at the time of the show—a fact that makes their childlessness that much more puzzling and the show's title, *The Honeymooners*, more than a touch ironic and possibly a shade bitter.

But however evasive the actual time of the series may be, what seems clear is that it is not the 1950s as most of the United States knew it. As Ron Simon wrote in *Television Quarterly* in 2005, the series takes no part in the postwar prosperity that characterized the families on television. Ozzie and Harriet Nelson, the Andersons of *Father Knows Best*, and the Cleavers of *Leave it to Beaver*

lived in the tree-lined, secure suburbs, all enjoying the material emblems of the American Dream. By 1955, even the prototypical proletariat family, the Goldbergs, had moved out of the city, from the Bronx to suburban bliss in Haverville. The Kramdens were the exception. Ralph and his suffering wife, Alice, were stuck in the urban wilderness—a cold-water apartment above a noisy New York street, without any creature comforts of Eisenhower conformity. Their main possessions were a plain dining table and a depression icebox.... The couples were childless in a baby boom USA.... the two icons of fifties America, the car and the home, were absent from Honeymoonerland.[17]

The decade of *The Honeymooners*, then, is not the 1950s in which it was broadcast but the difficult years of the Great Depression in which Gleason was a young man. Gleason's father, a white-collar worker in an insurance office—a reasonably good job arranged for him by his brother—continued to fall further and further behind before disappearing in 1925, leaving Mae as a single mother to face the bleakest years. Something like that desperation wells up in Gleason's character, but there is never a hint of surrender on the part of Ralph Kramden. His frustration is merely made more acute because he realizes his inability to provide well for Alice, whom he loves.

The Irish-American community may not have been hit any harder than the rest of the country, but the Irish-American experience of those years was inflected in a different way. It was in the 1930s that the long chain of serial migration from Ireland snapped and when the drying up of a stream of new immigrants and remittances weakened transatlantic links. As Stephen Erie and others have shown, the New Deal disrupted the machine politics that placed the Irish at the top of the heap of urban politics.[18]

17. Ron Simon, "Ralph Kramden and *The Honeymooners* Turn the Big 5 o (Sort Of)," *Television Quarterly* 36, no. 1 (Fall 2005): 62.

18. On the Irish-American community in the Depression years, see Stephen Erie, *Rainbow's End: Irish-Americans and the Dilemmas of Urban Machine Politics, 1840–1985*

Above all, the fact that the Irish had worked so long and so hard to get where they were when the Depression hit made the decade acutely disappointing. Bitterness over having had the "land of opportunity" snatched away from them just as they were about to take up full privilege is one of the defining experiences of the Irish in this country—one that translates into a heritage of skepticism and fatalism, a "black Irish" temperament inescapable in Gleason's, and Ralph Kramden's, view of the world.

The climate that prevails in the Kramden household, if not exactly poverty, is surely one of scarcity. Alice, at least, is well aware of how fully she is missing out on the consumer paradise of postwar America: in one episode she mocks their flat as a sort of Disneyland, sarcastically telling Ralph that their icebox is "the enchanted kingdom." In the episode "Hello Mom," Alice ticks off the many common comforts missing from her life, among them a washing machine, an electric stove, a vacuum cleaner, and a telephone. Here, the disconnect in time is obvious. By 1955, a full 92 percent of American households owned a refrigerator, and 94 percent of American households had a telephone.[19] But the Kramdens, in the middle of the first city of the nation, did not.

The scarcity of their lives evokes the tenement life of the immigrant generations that Gleason's immigrant forbears would have known. It is not wholly resentful: the series contains an element of *nostalgie de la boue* as well. Gleason had a sentimental streak, seen in episodes like "Young at Heart," which ends with a virtual sermon about the joys of the good old days. When Ralph resists a modern convenience, it's always because it will upset the face-to-face bonds of community; when he needs a message from work, a coworker drops by. It is an intriguing and self-ironizing gesture that the very

---

(Berkeley: University of California Press, 1990); see also Matthew J. O'Brien, "Irishness in Great Britain and the United States: Transatlantic and Cross-Channel Migration Networks and Irish Ethnicity, 1920–90" (Ph.D. diss., University of Wisconsin, 2001), especially chaps. 1 and 2.

19. *Statistical Abstract of the United States* (Washington: Government Printing Office, 1955).

first episode of the Classic 39 is titled "TV or Not TV" and revolves around the deleterious effects of a television set that Ralph purchases (though by this time, more than half the nation's homes had already bought a set). Ralph eventually returns the set because he no longer sees his friends.

Splurging on a television set is an exception that Ralph and Alice could not afford. The Kramdens are barely making it. They are much less comfortable than the Nortons, whose upstairs apartment appears nicely furnished, the few times we see it (but only because the Nortons have purchased their furnishings on credit). From time to time, *The Honeymooners* gives us poignant glimpses of Ralph realizing his own shortcomings as a provider; an episode titled "Young Man with a Horn," in which he studies for a civil service exam (which he fails), is especially touching. In most episodes, he sees advancement as a matter of who you know—a bit of an Irish trait, confirmed by his father's work life—and he is acutely aware that he lacks the social connections to get a promotion. Most of the time, though, Ralph takes his poverty with a kind of stoicism, the best a guy like him could expect. Again and again, he says, "I'm just a bus driver."

A full third of the episodes involve Ralph's inept attempts at upward mobility. A famous episode is "The Golfer," in which he erroneously believes he's been invited to a round of golf at his boss's country club as a prelude to a promotion. Ralph and Norton try to learn the sport from an instruction manual. The ludicrous juxtaposition of Ralph togged out in a tam and tweeds while standing in his shabby apartment and clueless as to how the game is played displays his haplessness before the realities of class. Ralph, however, is convinced that class boundaries can be leapt. He unfailingly banks on the same strategy for escape: he is powerless to resist a get-rich-quick scheme.

Ralph is endlessly looking for easy money, and the idea of easy money is Ralph's default strategy for advancement. But it is a strategy scarcely confined to *The Honeymooners*. The prospect of sudden wealth deserves serious evaluation as an Irish motif. For centuries, it has also been bound up with a constellation of ideas about Irishness, and especially so in America, starting with the legendary "gold in the streets" stories of immigration. Leprechauns and their pots of gold help to define Irishness in American popular culture.[20] Lucky Charms cereal has been on the shelves since 1964; Disney's *Darby O'Gill and the Little People* has been a St. Patrick's Day staple since 1959,[21] and *Finian's Rainbow* of 1947 remains a frequently revived American musical comedy;[22] Ralph has much in common with the dreamy Irishman Finian McLonergan hoping to plant his pot of gold near Fort Knox. The pot of gold works its way into dozens of iterations. One ready example is the "sweeps": throughout much of the twentieth century, if you asked most Americans to fill in a missing word after "Irish," they would almost instantly answer, "sweepstakes." From 1930 forward, the Irish Hospital sweepstakes was not only the most well-known lottery in the world, but in many ways, smuggling and selling sweeps tickets was also one of the persisting ethnic activities that brought together the Irish diasporic community.[23]

George McManus's enormously successful comic "Bringing up Father," about Jiggs, a one-time bricklayer and his parvenu wife Maggie—which was at its peak popularity in the 1930s, the years when young Jack Gleason was coming of age—never makes clear how Jiggs came into his sudden riches, but the basic joke is that he is completely unprepared for wealth.[24] *The Honeymooners* tells that joke whenever Ralph thinks he is about to strike it rich, as when he

20. See James Silas Rogers, "Ignorable Irishry: Leprechauns and Postwar Satire," in *After the Flood: Irish America 1945–1960*, ed. James Silas Rogers and Matthew J. O'Brien (Dublin: Irish Academic Press, 2009), 146–59.

21. *Darby O'Gill and the Little People*, directed by Robert Stevenson (1959).

22. *Finian's Rainbow*, book by E. Y. Harburg and Fred Saidy; music and lyrics by Burton Lane and Yip Harburg; 1947.

23. See Marie Coleman, *The Irish Sweep: A History of the Irish Hospitals Sweepstake, 1930–87* (Dublin: University College Dublin Press, 2009).

24. See Charles Fanning, "George McManus and Irish America," *ImageTexT: Interdisciplinary Comics Studies* 7, no. 2, http://www.english.ufl.edu/imagetext/archives/v7_2/fanning/.

looks at their shabby apartment and tells Alice, "you won't believe how good this furniture will look in a Park Avenue house."

Nor have get-rich-quick schemes been forgotten when Ireland is represented on screen. *Waking Ned Devine*, about winning the lottery, was one of the sleeper hits of 1998. The notion finds its way into Jim Sheridan's *In America* of 2002, in which the African man next door who covers the hospital bill of the young people turns out to be a rich potentate in exile. One could extend the idea to include a number of Irish big-score heist films, such as *Intermission* and *When Brendan Met Trudy*, but even without them we can run off a list of films involving hare-brained money-making schemes: *Quackser Fortune Has a Cousin in the Bronx*; *The Halo Effect*; *The Van*; *Eat the Peach*; *An Everlasting Piece*; *Spin the Bottle*; and the young musicians trying to make it big in *The Commitments*.[25]

And Ralph gets it. If the only way that popular culture allowed for an Irish person—"a mope like me," as he says—to attain wealth was through sudden good fortune, a lucky break, then Ralph is determined not to miss that chance. He buys up a stock of useless kitchen gadgets and goes on television to sell them (where he freezes in front of the camera). He invests in a low-calorie pizzeria chain. He schemes to win the cash prize at a costume party. He buys raffle tickets. He enters talent contests and expects to be discovered by a Hollywood scout in a play at the Raccoon Lodge Hall. He finds a suitcase of money on the bus and does not return it (it turns out to be counterfeit, of course). He goes on a television quiz show called the *$99,000 Question*, washing out on the first question, naturally; when selected to appear on the show, he tells Alice, "I'm finally going to find my own Pot o' Gold."[26]

25. *Waking Ned Devine*, directed by Kirk Jones (1998); *In America*, directed by Jim Sheridan (2002); *Intermission*, directed by John Crowley (2003); *When Brendan Met Trudy*, directed by Kieron J. Walsh (2000); *Quackser Fortune Has a Cousin in the Bronx*, directed by Waris Hussein (1970); *The Halo Effect*, directed by Lance Daly (2004); *The Van*, directed by Stephen Frears (1996); *Eat the Peach*, directed by *Peter Ormrod* (1986); *An Everlasting Piece*, directed by Barry Levinson (2000); *Spin the Bottle*, directed by Ian Fitzgibbon (2004); *The Commitments*, directed by Alan Parker (1991).
26. One might argue that Gleason's own celebrated taste for the high life—on

Irish themes, attitudes, patterns of life, ways of imagining the world percolated into the creative processes of artists like Gleason and Carney and into the television personas that they created. These artists enact Irishness without naming it—even, it seems, when they are engaged in willfully excluding its overt markers. It is in moments like these that we see the potency of ethnicity as a "figure in the carpet" in so much of American popular culture.

Perhaps, then, it is no surprise that when Gleason died in 1987, his obituarist in *People* magazine referred to his career as "a grand Irish life."[27] And perhaps, too, it is not quite as ironic as it seems that 2005, the series' golden anniversary, gave rise to a by-all-accounts lamentable remake of *The Honeymooners*, conceived of and starring Cedric the Entertainer and an all-black ensemble, which was filmed chiefly at Ardmore Studios in County Wicklow, as well as on locations in and around Dublin—including O'Connell Street, dressed out to look like Manhattan.

The Jackie Gleason Show (1966–70), which aired from Miami Beach, the coffee cup from which he sipped in fact contained champagne—also extended the joke of sudden wealth.

27. Brad Darrach, "A Fond Goodbye to the Great One," *People* 28, no 2, July 13, 1987, http://www.people.com/people/archive/article/0,,20096724,00.html.

5

A Culture of Diffidence

Mid-Century Irish-American Priests' Autobiographies

Why are the autobiographies of priests and former priests consistently disappointing as literature and so rarely informative about the emotional lives of their authors? This chapter considers a number of such autobiographies, written before the Second Vatican Council by American priests of Irish descent—a time when the Irish experience of Catholicism was the most dominant thread in North America, and nowhere more so than among the Catholic intelligentsia. In the 1950s, priests were highly visible in the United States; by no means were they all intellectuals, but in terms of sheer numbers, America was home to more than 50,000 Catholic priests, of whom at least a third were of Irish descent.[1] After the council, a

An earlier version of this article appeared in *Studies: An Irish Quarterly Review* 96, no. 381 (Summer 2007), and is reprinted with permission.

1. *The Official Catholic Directory Anno Domini 1960* (New York: P. J. Kenedy and Sons, 1960) counted 54,682 ordained Catholic priests in the United States. In 1972, sociologist Andrew M. Greeley found that 35 percent of the American Catholic clergy were of Irish descent; Greeley, *That Most Distressful Nation: The Taming of the American Irish* (Chicago: Quadrangle, 1972), 93.

A Culture of Diffidence

short-lived but vigorous body of Catholic autobiography arose, and some of the insights that can be gleaned from that literature are also used here to illuminate pre-conciliar work.

Without being glib, one can say that in the 1960s, "self-disclosure" approached sacramental status for many American Catholics; the phenomena that informed this efflorescence ranged from the larger cultural interest in "encounter" and other growth psychologies to the serious theological engagement with Martin Buber's *I and Thou*.[2] And in the spirit of confessionalism, the 1960s witnessed a fair number of angry Catholic books; James Kavanaugh's bestselling *A Modern Priest Looks at his Outdated Church* (1967) was a classic grievance narrative.[3] Nonetheless, there was a brief post-Vatican II flourishing of autobiography that had its roots in a sincere conviction that Catholic personalism, with its stress on the unique experiences of persons, provided a welcome, necessary validation of individual experience. Many in the American church embraced, or at least tried to embrace, a new willingness to share their personal witness and experience by Catholic thinkers. Thinking on "the pilgrim church" translated, on an individual level, to a trust in the value of telling one's own journey.

But what of the decade before the Second Vatican Council? Did the religious men of postwar America produce a comparable body of first-person writing? Given the central importance of vocations to the Irish-American family (the stereotypical mother giving her pride and joy to God), the extraordinary social and political influence of priests on Irish-American life, and the fact that virtually all of these priests were college graduates and thus literate men whom we would expect to be both personally and professionally interested

2. Martin Buber, *I and Thou* (New York: Charles Scribner and Sons, 1937). By the end of the decade, the enthusiasm in Catholic circles for a psychologically informed self-disclosure was shown in the immensely popular success of John Powell, SJ's *Why Am I Afraid to Tell You Who I Am?* (Niles, Ill.: Argus Communications, 1969), which has now sold more than 15 million copies. It was a frequent text in the Catholic secondary classrooms of the 1970s.

3. James A. Kavanaugh, *A Modern Priest Looks at His Outdated Church* (New York: Trident, 1967).

in the interior life, it seems reasonable to expect a significant body of autobiographical literature by priests.

Additionally, one might have expected support among publishers for such works in the wake of the astonishing success of Thomas Merton's *The Seven Storey Mountain* (1948), which sold more than 600,000 copies in its first year.[4] Bishop Fulton J. Sheen's run as a television celebrity from 1952 through 1957 demonstrated that there was a popular market for things Catholic. Indeed, in the 1950s, American popular culture was in many ways fascinated with the figure of the priest: in addition to Merton and Sheen, the best-selling novel of 1950 was *The Cardinal*, Karl Malden's portrayal of Fr. Corrigan in *On the Waterfront* was nominated for an Oscar in 1954, and J. F. Powers's priest stories in the *New Yorker* enjoyed critical and popular success.[5] In other words, the pieces were in place for a significant body of first-person literature by priests to have emerged.

The reality, unfortunately, is that this is an impoverished body of literature. Autobiographies by any stripe of Catholic—Irish or not, ordained or otherwise—were exceedingly rare in the years preceding Vatican II. The bimonthly trade publication *Catholic Book Merchandiser*, each issue of which included brief descriptions of new titles in American Catholic publishing, did not list "autobiography" as a separate category: memoirs and the like were subsumed into the category of biography. That category overwhelmingly comprised lives of the saints and popes. Of 315 new or forthcoming biographies listed from 1960 to 1962 (the years on the eve of the Council) only thirty-six titles, or slightly more than 11 percent, were autobiographies by living authors—and that allows for the broadest possible definition of Catholic autobiography.[6]

4. Thomas Merton, *The Seven Storey Mountain* (New York: Harcourt Brace, 1948).

5. Henry Morton Robinson, *The Cardinal* (New York: Simon and Schuster, 1950); *On the Waterfront*, directed by Elia Kazan (1954); Powers's stories are collected in J. F. Powers, *Prince of Darkness and Other Stories* (Garden City, N.Y.: Doubleday, 1947) and *The Presence of Grace* (Garden City, N.Y.: Doubleday, 1956).

6. Many of the books listed are accounts of escape from Iron Curtain countries. I have counted each reissue of Dr. Tom Dooley's works as a new book. The

A Culture of Diffidence

Further, those few priests' memoirs that did find their way into print in the pre–Vatican II years are characterized by a marked lack of self-disclosure. Sometimes pietistic, sometimes preoccupied with doctrinal argument, and sometimes marked by a faux intimacy of the affable, Pat O'Brien–sort of way, the inner—and much of the external—lives of the clerics who wrote these books remained uncharted.

Cardinal Cushing of Boston once observed that he had never met an American bishop who was not the son of a laboring man. Despite his claim, the Irish-American priest-memoirists considered here rarely dwell on their parent's poverty, and in the case of James Keller's *To Light a Candle* (1963), the family lived in comparative affluence; his immigrant father was a thriving dry goods merchant.[7] However, in *Yankee Priest*, Fr. Edward Murphy's on-the-whole enjoyable 1950 account of growing up in turn-of-the-century Massachusetts, his father's poverty is clear: "Dad . . . never received more than eight or ten dollars a week for the sweat of his brow, though he toiled like a Trojan under a Greek at any honest job that offered. Nothing was too menial for him."[8] Daniel Berrigan's much later autobiography, *To Dwell in Peace* (1987),[9] also makes much of his father's economic misfortunes.

Much more striking, to a contemporary reader, is the silence concerning the emotional dynamics of the families described. In Gerard McGinley's *A Trappist Writes Home* (1960),[10] there is not a sin-

"Catholic authors" represented include singer Kate Smith, actress Loretta Young, and baseball player Frankie Frisch, as well as such frivolous titles as Mimi Rhea, *I Was Jacqueline Kennedy's Dressmaker* (New York: Popular Library, 1963).

7. James Keller, *To Light a Candle: The Autobiography of James Keller, Founder of the Christophers* (Garden City, N.Y.: Doubleday, 1963).

8. Edward F. Murphy, *Yankee Priest: An Autobiographical Journey, with Certain Detours, from Salem to New Orleans* (Garden City, N.Y.: Doubleday, 1952), 10.

9. Daniel Berrigan, *To Dwell in Peace: An Autobiography* (San Francisco: Harper and Row, 1987). At one point, Berrigan says of his father that "He was a failure in the eyes of others; and inevitably, in his own. He would never write the Irishman's version of the American dream"; Berrigan, *To Dwell*, 19.

10. Gerard McGinley, *A Trappist Writes Home: Letters of Abbot Gerard McGinley, OCSO, to his Family* (Milwaukee: Bruce, 1960).

gle mention of the author's earthly father or mother, only letter after letter on the glories of devotion. In *The Bishop Jots It Down: An Autobiographical Strain on Words*—a title that announces his reticence at the start—Bishop Francis Clement Kelley of Oklahoma City makes no allusion to his mother, and practically none to his father beyond remarking than to say that he was "a man of few words."[11]

One pattern that clearly seems to obtain in these autobiographies is that the mother is usually the stronger presence in the home and in the lives of the boys. Admittedly, the experiences of these few Irish Americans may not necessarily be distinct from those of any other cohort of young men growing up in industrializing, early-twentieth century America—but forceful paternal presences are scarce. James Keller says of his father, "Because his work kept him away from home the greater part of the day and into the evening, it fell to Mother to become not only the directing head of the household in his absence but also the moving spirit."[12] In *Yankee Priest*, Murphy says of his mother's authority, "Never for a moment did she not let Dad feel that he was master of the home; but never was master more effectively mistressed."[13] Berrigan, writing in a later and more reflective time, poignantly says of his youth that "The worst of all times are synonymous with my mother's absence.... Childhood or adolescence, it makes little difference: deprived of her, the house is an empty vessel, a tomb."[14]

Another telling note: the most consistent pattern in the accounts of their families is that the priest-biographers rarely refer to their siblings. Other than passing references to brothers and sisters, siblings are consistently left out of their stories. The young lives of these priests appear almost entirely oriented toward the adult world. In light of the strong mothers and the seemingly weak sibling bonds, it is tempting to speculate on the part that surrogacy,

---

11. Francis Clement Kelley, *The Bishop Jots It Down: An Autobiographical Strain on Words* (1939; New York, Harper, 1948). Note the central place of reticence in the title.

12. Keller, *To Light*, 15. 13. Murphy, *Yankee Priest*, 11.

14. Berrigan, *To Dwell*, 23.

or what we might today call "father hunger," plays in these autobiographies.[15] In virtually every story of vocation, an affirming, welcoming cleric is remembered with gratitude. These priest-memoirists may or may not have had a distinct experience of fathers, but they had an exceptional experience of having been mentored.

A pattern of reticence about their family of origin, coupled with extensive memory-sharing about their boarding educations, inevitably leads to the speculation that for these men, the seminary at least partially substituted for the family. And if, as the literature hints, ordinary familial bonding was interrupted or did not "take," that may help us to understand another theme that recurs in this literature: the frequent sense of standing apart, of being unlike others. Some of these priests go to great lengths to demonstrate their average boyhoods by telling of their love of baseball, their petty infractions that found them hauled before the pastor or principal, or their hatred of the Saturday evening bath. Notably, in many priests' autobiographies, there is also an episode or moment in which they are singled out or come to think of themselves as apart from the others in their world. Even Bishop Sheen, who was nothing if not self-assured, makes jokes about the torment of going to school with an odd name like "Fulton" and mentions in *Treasure in Clay* (1980) that—unlike the rest of his family—he realized early he was not cut out for farm work.[16]

There was, of course, a widespread belief that, by virtue of their vocation and the small and not-so-small renunciations expected of the ordained, priests were different from other men. While more polemic than autobiography, James Kavanaugh's book nonetheless discloses something of its author's young life. He describes the

15. An extensive popular and professional literature has developed concerning the concept of "father hunger" among American men, the most influential of which is Robert Bly, *Iron John: A Book about Men* (Reading, Mass.: Addison-Wesley, 1990).

16. Fulton Sheen, *Treasure in Clay: The Autobiography of Fulton J. Sheen* (Garden City, N.Y.: Image, 1982), 8. Though Sheen was a celebrity, his autobiography was not published until after his death. Sheen, incidentally, was a great raconteur of Irish stories, which were collected in a video and DVD titled, *Bishop Fulton J. Sheen: His Irish Wit and Wisdom* (Vision Video, 2006 [DVD]) that sells briskly today.

summer of his entry into the seminary as a teenager in the latter years of World War II:

> I would never be the same again, since I had decided to be a priest. I was never to date, was to avoid movies, beaches and mixed parties, and to attend Mass every day, meditate every morning of my life, and select a summer job which would not jeopardize my special call.... My father told me I was too serious, my mother said that I had lost my personality and spark. There were explosions in the summer when tensions ran too high.... I was exempted from the service by the importance of my work and felt cowardly and less a man when I talked to my former classmates in the Army or Marines.... but I was a seminarian, a chosen man, the pride of the parish, the future leader of our Church. And I was indescribably alone.[17]

In this context, one intriguing incident in James Keller's memoir may take on deeper significance:

> When I was about five years old, a friend of Mother's jokingly asked her if she had adopted me. I suppose I was a bit of a contrast, being slight and dark while all the other children were sturdy and fair. To my childish ears, though, that remark was not the slightest bit amusing. It was a deadly serious piece of news. I remember to this day how distressed and lost I felt. I felt as if I didn't belong here ... if this wasn't my family ... how did I get here and where *did* I belong? I began to look at my brothers and sisters with a sort of awe; they were the real thing—I was the intruder. This went on for several days until mother must have noticed that something was bothering me. She took me in her lap and said something like, "What's the matter my little Jamie?" After sobbing out my troubled heart, she gave me the reassurance I had been longing for.[18]

Perhaps a story that a million other boys could tell; but perhaps, especially because of its anomalous relationship to the otherwise guarded rest of the book, Keller is here suggesting a deeper psychic homelessness.

For Edward Murphy, the sense of standing apart is tied explic-

17. Kavanaugh, *Modern Priest*, 19.
18. Keller, *To Light*, 15–16; ellipses in original.

itly to a familiar, even stereotypical, icon of rising Irish social status: a piano in the parlor. It was a beat-up old piano that his workingman father bought secondhand from the Father Mathew Hall, and he recalls, "Now we Murphys had something that most other families lacked."[19] But there is an interesting gender dimension in the story: when his sister Annie, for whom the piano had been purchased, injured her hand in a biscuit-making machine, Edward was pressed into taking piano lessons two hours a day. One can hear the exclusion in his story:

And that was how one phase of my boyhood ended. . . . Gone was a large portion of my freedom to skip off to the ever fascinating waves that washed the shore; and worse beyond words, I was now shunned by most of the neighborhood boys, to whom even the beginning of such sissiness as piano playing was the same as smallpox.[20]

We read such passages with an assumption of intended irony, imagining the bemused avuncularity of the adult looking back. But the tone changes completely if we read it straight. In that case, we must take seriously the assertion that this young man who became a priest, was—in his formative years—compelled by familial duty to ignore conventional gender roles and was mocked as a result.

A clear and persuasive portrait of its subject's youthful sense of disconnection appears in Donald Hayne's 1963 *Batter My Heart*, in which the author—who was in and out of seminaries and dioceses all his life—speaks quite openly about his realization at about age fifteen that he is homosexual.[21] Actually, Hayne soft-pedals any distress that this realization caused him (as did his confessor, whom Hayne says responded with "derisive hooting when I told him so").[22] The author resolves to live a life of absolute celibacy.

19. Murphy, *Yankee Priest*, 22. For a brilliant discussion of the piano's iconic significance in Irish-American life, see Ron Ebest, *Private Histories: The Writing of Irish Americans, 1900–1935* (Notre Dame: University of Notre Dame Press, 2005), 57–76.

20. Murphy, *Yankee Priest*, 24.

21. Donald Hayne, *Batter My Heart* (New York: Knopf, 1963).

22. Ibid., 35.

Much more distressing to Hayne than his sexuality is the awkward reality that his parents were separated: he grows adept at masking this family secret in school, telling teachers and classmates that his father is simply "away"—and even more so, hiding what he recalls as "my constant shame at his profession of gambling."[23]

Born in Albany in 1908, Hayne's childhood more than fulfills the suggestion of strong maternal influence found in the other books. His father was a sporadic presence at best; actually, he was spending part of the time in prison. Hayne and his mother lived in a big Victorian home that belonged to his aunts, the five spinster sisters of the Mullen family—who had disapproved of his mother's marriage in the first place and in fact disapproved of all marriages on principle. Nonetheless, his parents make attempts to reconcile. Sometimes his mother goes to Saratoga or Belmont racetracks with his father. "She would come back," he writes, "with descriptions, half contemptuous, half amused, of the people she had seen as though they were creatures from another planet. To her, with the Irish Catholic Mullens of Third Street behind her, they were."[24] A feminized Irish Catholic obsession with the appearance of propriety steeps the household in which Hayne was raised. In one sad incident, two young curates from nearby St. Joseph's rectory begin dropping in frequently for coffee and cake with his mother—only to run afoul of neighborhood gossip and be banned from visiting by the pastor.

The adult Hayne reflects that he grew up in this environment intuiting that in his life, "I had two big jobs to do: to keep my father's weakness from ever cropping out in me, and to give my mother all the love she deserved, for all the sacrifices she had made for me."[25] And again, one cannot help but wonder if the author's vocation—helped along the way by a succession of vivid intellectual mentors—is not in some way the story of his search for the good father.

23. Ibid., 38.   24. Ibid., 39.
25. Ibid., 7.

A Culture of Diffidence

Batter My Heart is quite an unusual book. Reading it today, one senses that the blurb on its dust jacket about how he "dared to question his Church and to follow his heart into a harrowing search for truth and peace" may be true at some level—but also that at other levels, Hayne was one of those incredibly needy, high-maintenance personalities who must have driven his bishops batty. As the story unfolds, he enters academic life, loses his faith by reading in logical positivism, dabbles in Eastern religion, undergoes analysis, and goes to Hollywood and becomes Cecil B. DeMille's personal secretary (which led to a small speaking role in *The Ten Commandments*—although few Americans have heard of Hayne, millions have actually heard him, as his is the Voice of God in that movie). Later he flirts with Episcopalianism and, eventually, returns to the Catholic Church.

Hayne neither surrenders to the smugness of earlier priests' autobiographies nor indulges in the wearying bitterness of so many that followed. To be sure, much of the memoir is tediously cerebral, and there are important parts that fall well short of full disclosure. For instance, we get only a few hints about how, while still a priest, he fell in love and started a sexual relationship with a young woman whom he was assigned to counsel, being kissed for the first time at age thirty-two. Later, his close friendship with Christopher Isherwood in California makes no reference to the latter's gay lifestyle. And though Hayne married in 1949, fathered two children, and divorced in 1958, that part of his life is treated in less than one page. Yet for all of the gaps, there is risk-taking and intimacy in his story.

In contrast, other mid-century priests' autobiographies provide little of what we now expect from life-writing—such simple things as the rendering of a historical milieu, the probing of formative events, even the simple effort of reflection. We expect autobiographies to be "personal"; but that was not how priests had been taught to conceive of their lives. One could posit several explanations for this striking reluctance to disclose.

The practice of frequent confession almost certainly played a role in inhibiting Catholic autobiography, though there is much to suggest that the sacrament was usually approached within the "manualist tradition"—the so-called laundry list of sins—and rarely treated as an occasion for a probing self-examination. Still, there can be no doubt that for many, the sacrament gave Catholics an alternative space in which to voice their secrets. Indirectly, the Catholic practice of frequent confession worked against autobiography by subverting the innately triumphalist character of the genre. Autobiography is almost always about success; even when the author is writing of personal misfortunes and mistakes, there is an implicit success story about the lessons learned or about converting unhappiness into a work. Frequent confession, however, reminds the writer that he or she is almost certain to fail again. To write an autobiography, in such a schema, is to risk the sin of presumption.

Additionally, we must situate this literature in the larger context of mid-twentieth-century America—the famous "Gray Flannel Suit" of the conformist Eisenhower years, described by the sociologist David Reisman as a time when Americans backed away from individualism in favor of an "other-directedness" that was more at ease in a corporate environment in which expected roles were clear and impersonal.[26] There is considerable anecdotal evidence that mid-century American Catholics thrived in organizations like the military, the FBI, and IBM owing to their familiarity with the definitively hierarchical organization of the church itself. Indeed, in precisely the years described by the autobiographies considered here, many intellectuals were aghast at the supposed regimentation of Catholics in America.[27]

26. David Reisman, *The Lonely Crowd: A Study in the Changing American Character* (New Haven: Yale University Press, 1950).

27. A thorough discussion of the perception that the Catholic familiarity with hierarchical, even collectivist, institutions rendered the group inimical to American individualism is found in John T. McGreevy, "Thinking on One's Own: Catholicism in the American Intellectual Imagination, 1928–1960," *Journal of American History* 84, no. 1 (June 1997): 97–131. I noted the Catholic overrepresentation in hierarchical organizations in "The Green in the Gray Flannel Suit," unpublished paper presented at the American Conference for Irish Studies annual meeting (April, 2006), University of Missouri-St. Louis. The soft-pedaling of individualism—to put it mildly!—can surely also be linked to the paucity of autobiography.

A Culture of Diffidence

To turn to a more specifically Catholic context, there was an ingrained distrust of conversion narratives as a distinctly Protestant form, St. Augustine and St. Paul notwithstanding. Perhaps the stress placed on the canonized saints also dampened the willingness of unassuming Catholics to put their own lives on public display; seminary training emphasized obedience and meekness. In 1974, Wilfred Sheed published a short survey of the post–Vatican II moment in the United States in which he found the failure of autobiography to be symptomatic of what was then American Catholicism's unexpectedly sudden malaise. In part, Sheed ascribes this to the vigorous enforcement of humility upon Catholics, a virtue that he describes as having been "dumped over us like water on a hysteric, leaving us soggy and irritable, or passive, as the case may be." The result is a lasting gap in the written record. "One reason," he concludes, "we never get this historically valuable testimony is that American Catholics have more than usual difficulty with the first person, using it flippantly or defiantly or not at all."[28] For the vast majority of priests—including, in many ways, even those priests whose memoirs did find their way into a book—their understanding of what humility meant led to choosing the option of "not at all."

The paucity of intimacy and cultural context in this literature is also linked to the fact that, in the Catholic literary tradition, the place of autobiography had unfailingly been located in the intellect. Conversion narratives by Catholics stressed the intellectual irresistibility of Catholic argument, and nowhere more so in the work of John Henry Newman, whose 1865 *Apologia Pro Vita Sua* was a definitive Catholic autobiography.[29] It is, above all, a narrative of intellectual surrender to the propositions of Catholicism. It is certainly not a story of personal engagement; as Newman asserted, "From the time that I became a Catholic, of course, I have no further history of my religious opinions to narrate."[30]

28. Wilfred Sheed, *Three Mobs: Labor, Church and Mafia* (New York: Sheed and Ward, 1974), 115.
29. John Henry Newman, *Apologia Pro Vita Sua* (New York: Longmans, 1908).
30. Ibid., 238.

A Culture of Diffidence

It need hardly be said that by no stretch of the imagination could the priest memoirists discussed here be considered Newman's equal in terms of intellect or eloquence. And yet, the postconversion reticence of Newman's remark would have been readily embraced by the Irish-American priests of fifty to a hundred years later. They had all come of age in a culture of diffidence.

Flowering Absences

Recent Irish Writers and Genealogical Dead Ends

Julia Watson, in "Ordering the Family: Genealogy as Autobiographical Pedigree," offers a harsh, but defensible characterization of genealogical practice as it has traditionally been conducted. In the course of discussing those family history researchers who seek to "complete" an individual's family tree in exhaustive detail, Watson writes,

Part of the lure of genealogy is that it charts a linear history foregrounding lineage as pedigree. It emphasizes the family's sense of the stability and the "cleanness" of its ethnic composition, its maintenance of or "improvement" in social class, and the perpetuation from generation to generation of identified social institutions—religion, the professions, the production of heirs. Who begat whom, where, and in what line is knowledge that secures a patriarchal mooring in an increasingly destabilized world.[1]

An earlier version of this chapter appeared in "New Approaches to Family History, Genealogy and Irish-American Studies," in *Working Papers in Irish Studies* (Fort Lauderdale: Department of Liberal Arts, Nova Southeastern University, 2002), and is reprinted with permission.
    1. Julia Watson, "Ordering the Family: Genealogy as Autobiographical Pedi-

Watson is certainly correct that the concept of genealogy as "credentialing"—in many cases, a sort of trophy hunting that seeks to turn lineage into undisputed virtue—continues to exert a powerful influence. One of the most well-known Irish poems that concerns descent, Yeats's "Pardon Old Fathers," in which he praises the "Merchant and scholar who have left me blood / That has not passed through any huckster's loin"[2] was written "precisely to assert the respectability of the author's progenitors," in response to a snub by George Moore.[3] In America, such groups as the Daughters of the American Revolution, for instance (which often had their origins in the anti-immigrant nativism of the nineteenth century) were well on their way to being moribund until the Civil Rights Movement gave them a huge recruiting boost. Genealogical braggadocio was a staple in the bombast of earlier Irish-American authors—most notably Michael O'Brien, an amateur historian who ransacked colonial American records to turn up evidence of venerable, and therefore upright, Irish antecedents.[4]

For many recent creative writers, however, genealogy is a more nuanced undertaking. For these writers, the impulse to explore one's line of descent is bound up with a larger process of establishing their own sense of self as an artist. The contributions of poets and memoirists to a creative literature of genealogy help to reframe the ways in which we may understand the investigation of family and ancestry. In their hands, genealogy is not a gesture of self-importance, but rather a way of knowing and a means to approach complex human experiences and emotions. This chapter consid-

---

gree," in *Getting a Life: Everyday Uses of Autobiography*, ed. Sidonie Smith and Julia Watson (Minneapolis: University of Minnesota Press, 1996), 307.

2. William Butler Yeats, "Pardon Old Fathers," in *Selected Poems and Four Plays of William Butler Yeats*, ed. M. L. Rosenthal (New York: Scribner's, 1996), 38.

3. A. Norman Jeffares, *A New Commentary on the Poems of W. B. Yeats* (Stanford: Stanford University Press, 1984), 98–102.

4. Michael J. O'Brien (1870–1960), a Catholic priest who was deeply involved with the American Irish Historical Society, wrote dozens of books and articles, the best known of which is probably *A Hidden Phase of American History: Ireland's Part in America's Struggle for Liberty* (New York: Dodd, Mead, 1919).

Flowering Absences

ers how four contemporary Irish poets—John Montague, Michael Coady, Eavan Boland, and Chris Arthur—and one Irish-American poet, Brendan Galvin, articulate expansive and original conceptions of the genealogical project. There is a transatlantic dimension to the work of Montague and Coady; the former was born in Brooklyn (the title of his collection of autobiographical essays), and the latter's researches brought him to Philadelphia.

Of the authors discussed here, Coady is easily the most preoccupied with ancestry and descent. In a memorable reflection on the pursuit, Coady writes that "the purpose of genealogy should not be the neat assembly of pedigree, culminating smugly in self, but its exact opposite: the extension of the personal beyond the self to encounter the intimate unknown of others in our blood."[5]

Unlike the models of genealogy that place the individual at the teleological endpoint of an unbroken line of succession, the recent literature of genealogy has little to do with filling in the gaps in a family tree. Rather, it finds its subject matter in dead ends, dislocation, and a sense of loss; in coming, as Mississippi-born John Bentley Mays wrote in his genealogical memoir *Power in the Blood*, "to the end of the road and of history, to the clearing surrounded by impenetrable forests of forgetfulness."[6]

The literature of genealogy lives in the place of unanswered questions or, more precisely, in the place where the author recognizes that such unanswered questions can nonetheless give rise to an imaginative response—a phenomenon that John Montague has termed "A Flowering Absence." Montague's seventeen-stanza poem of this title, from his 1984 collection *The Dead Kingdom*,[7] charts an autobiographical journey that runs from abandonment through an attempt to confront the fact of his mother's neglect, into shame and inarticulate stammering, on to the healing, closing lines in which "the sweet oils of poetry" bring ease and light to the faltering poet.

5. Michael Coady, *All Souls* (Oldcastle, County Meath: Gallery, 1997), 89.

6. John Bentley Mays, *Power in the Blood: Land, Memory, and a Southern Family* (New York: HarperCollins, 1996), 76.

7. John Montague, *The Dead Kingdom* (Oxford: Oxford University Press, 1984).

The poem is featured again in Montague's 1991 gathering-together of autobiographical poetry and essays *Born in Brooklyn*,[8] a title that underscores the mature poet's preoccupation with origins.

In Montague's case, his sense of dislocation from family history is more a matter of feeling that he is an emotional orphan than of being ignorant of his past. His line of descent is fully charted; he knows his parents and knows where they were (and where they were not) during his earliest years. In that sense, it may seem a stretch to read "A Flowering Absence" as a genealogical poem—but it is a work that outlines, if not his family, then at least his artistic origins, which are intimately bound up in the poet's wrenching early removal from his mother. Despite Montague's knowledge of the generations that preceded him, "A Flowering Absence" is clearly a poem suffused with a sense of genealogical inquiry. Montague writes, "Year by year, I track it down / intent for a hint of evidence."[9] Later, when he recalls the immigrant wet nurses who looked after him, nameless then and now, he writes, "I bless their unrecorded names." This act—blessing the unnamed, making an absence flower—reprises the promise of the poem's title.

Stanzas five through seven touch most clearly on Montague's search for "roots." In these lines, Montague sets off for the hospital where he was born, hoping to recover something of his lineage of abandonment, and suggests that the speaker looks on this as entering an underworld (the subway, Virgil, "darkest Brooklyn"). The outcome of the trip is an experience common among family historians:

> I took the subway to the hospital
> in darkest Brooklyn, to call
> on the old nun who nursed you
> through the travail of my birth
> to come on another cold trail.

8. Montague, *Born in Brooklyn: John Montague's America*, ed. David Lampe (Fredonia, N.Y.: White Pine Press, 1991).

9. Montague, "A Flowering Absence," in *Born in Brooklyn*, 21–23.

Flowering Absences

He then quotes the response of the nuns at the hospital:

Sister Virgillius, how strange!
She died just before you came.
She was delirious, rambling of all
her old patients; she could well
have remembered your mother's name.[10]

It is good to remember that Montague's poem, at the same time as it records the frustration of losing the trail, also reminds us that a skeletal genealogy, a listing of names on a page, would be only a cold comfort. Had the nun merely remembered his mother's name it would not have sufficed to heal Montague's emotional loss; her name, unlike those of the immigrant wet nurses who actually did nurture him, has been recorded and known all along. The person who could possibly have given the desired note of connection is dead and gone, having been snatched away just a short time before. Montague may know the lineaments of his inheritance, but a cul-de-sac keeps him from taking rest there; and it is his willingness to admit to the enduring potency of that interrupted inquiry that gives rise to some of his most moving poetic reckonings.

A genealogical account that moves to a more fully realized conclusion is Michael Coady's remarkable 1997 volume *All Souls*.[11] A montage of poetry, documentation, and prose (some written in the person of his vanished ancestors), *All Souls* closes with a fifty-page memoir titled "The Use of Memory" that chronicles Coady's historical recovery—albeit a fragmented and sketchy recovery—of his great-grandfather.

Coady has lived all his life in Carrick-on-Suir, Tipperary, as have at least five generations before him, with the notable exception of James Coady, who lived from 1848 to 1915. He was an illiterate boatman on the River Suir who abandoned his family in 1881 and vanished into the immigrant slums of America—specifically, as Coady eventually learns, in Philadelphia. One of several ironies

10. Ibid., 22.
11. See note 5.

in the family story is its reversal of the usual pattern of genealogical pursuit: his is the story of a resident of Ireland sifting through archives and census rolls in the New World. In other ways, though, the research trail that Coady chronicles differs little from that of thousands of researchers in America and other diasporic communities. The centrality of interruption as a theme in the genealogical quest is underscored by an event in Coady's book that exactly replicates Montague's story. Years earlier, he had heard from his mother that an elderly woman once mentioned something about his great-grandfather's second marriage in America. Coady tracks her down, but the old lady slips into a coma just before he can interview her. Such incidents play a large part in creating a sense of urgency that suffuses so many genealogical memoirs. The writer comes to realize that the past is a wasting asset, eroded further by each death in the family and by every generation that neglects to inquire into its own history.

Coady's re-creation of the story of his vanished ancestor provides an elaborate annotation of his poem "The Letter," first published in 1987.[12] The defining moment of the story is precisely an interruption in the record: some thirty years after leaving Ireland, the poet's grandfather received a letter from the New World in which the father tried to reestablish contact with the son he had cruelly abandoned years earlier. The son would have none of it; he tears up the letter and dashes it into the fire, and never again speaks of the incident. As Coady's poem describes the scene, he imagines his vanished ancestor as *"an old man / in some room in Philadelphia / reaching for words to bridge / the ocean of his silence"* and addresses this imagined figure with sympathy:

> *Silence was the bitter*
> *answer you were given*
> *every empty day until you died:*

---

12. Coady, "The Letter," in *Oven Lane* (Oldcastle: Gallery, 1987), 26–30. The poem carries the dedication "For James Coady, lost father of my grandfather." It is reprinted in the preface to the essay "The Use of Memory" in *All Souls*, 83–84.

Flowering Absences

by a breakfast table
my child father
watched your son unseal
his darkest pain

saw the pages torn and cast
in mortal grief and anger
out of an abandoned child's
unspeakable heart hunger
into the brute finality
of flame.[13]

This tragic story provides the crucial theme of Coady's work: he finds his creative wellspring by looking into that absence. He recalls his working and reworking of the poem that would later become a book:

Every writer knows the mysterious addition of unexpected things emerging on the page. As I wrote my way through its drafts, the poem became more than the exploratory articulation of the family narrative, with its mystery and pain; its writing discovered something else in the process: some paradigm for the mystery of the written word itself. I was invoking a poem of reconciliation within which I was also explicitly present as a writer, scripting the poem I invoked. As my great-grandfather in America had once bent over the blank page, so I found myself struggling to reply with words upon a page, three generations on.[14]

Having only scant data, but with determination and a series of contacts that seem providential in their helpfulness, Coady embarks on a genealogical search that eventually brings him to find his great-grandfather's unmarked grave and to confront at least some of the gaps in this fractured family story.

As he probes the missing chapters in the family story, in which "Intuition was straining toward fact in the manner of poet Michael Hartnett's wonderful phrase, 'I can foretell the past,'"[15] Coady

13. Coady, *All Souls*, 84.   14. Ibid., 93.
15. Ibid., 103.

makes creative leaps across the unrecorded generations that give reality and substance to his narrative. For instance, when he learns that his grandfather's death certificate records alcoholism and a broken hip, Coady writes, "As though a button had been pressed, my imagination instantly 'foretold' the past in flashback: a man too old for waterfront work, staggering and falling in an alleyway at night and lying there unheeded until morning."[16]

Coady in no way privileges the "factual" record over those places in the story in which he must tap into his writerly imagination. "It was," he writes, "a search in which creative hypothesis was necessarily often invoked along with the systematic combing of street directories, census records, newspapers, indexes of births, marriages, deaths."[17] He even coins the word *presequence* to describe his "knowing return to a seminal moment in the past from its own future."[18] In Coady's genealogical detective story, he insists that a writer's ability to envision the past is a legitimate epistemology. Coady would agree with the Alabama writer Dennis Covington that "the writer has another eye . . . that casts its pale sorrowful light backward over the past and forward into the future, akin in everything at once, the whole story, from beginning to end."[19]

At first glance, the work of Eavan Boland would seem to have little to do with the literature of genealogy; no impulse to retrieve a particular family history shapes her oeuvre. Yet, if we look on the genealogical project as a matter of looking closely at the discontinuities in the received account of the past and of having confidence in a writer's ability to re-create the past, then Boland's insistence that we not confuse what was recorded and handed with what actually happened is a crucial point. The past, to Boland, is always

---

16. Ibid., 116.   17. Ibid., 102.
18. Ibid., 88.

19. Dennis Covington, *Salvation on Sand Mountain: Snake-Handling and Redemption in Southern Appalachia* (Reading, Mass: Addison-Wesley, 1995), 175. Covington's book about the bizarre religious practice of snake-handling eventually morphs into a sort of family history as he discovers that several of his forebears were snakehandlers.

a shadowy place. And it is the vast, potent uncertainty of the past that spurs her distrust of the "official" record. Her poetic reclamation of the Famine's legacy, in particular, has compelled Boland to think deeply on the silence that has attended this horrific event: "A silence in which stories were not told, in which memories were not handed on, in which the ordinary sorrow and devastation of a people was neither named nor recorded."[20]

A willingness to trust the writer's own imagination and to validate the imagination as a rightful way of knowing the unrecorded past is central to Boland's practice in her 1996 collection *Object Lessons*.[21] That milestone work opens with Boland imaginatively reconstructing her grandmother's entry, in October 1909, into the National Maternity Hospital, a hospitalization in which she died. Boland has no qualms about confabulating that which is not recorded to history, about filling in gaps with imagined "facts" that give detail and life to events known only in outline:

This is the way we make the past. This is the way I will make her. Listening for hooves. Glimpsing the red hat which was never there in the first place. Giving eyesight and evidence to a woman we never knew and cannot now recover. And for all our violations, the past waits for us.[22]

Later, in "The Woman, the Place, the Poet," Boland extends her project of genealogical filling-in when she visits Clonmel, County Tipperary, and the ruins of a workhouse (as well as the still-used hospital that occupies the site today). Her great-grandfather had served as master of this "total institution." As she leaves its dark rooms,

I came out into sunshine. Poetic license in an age-old concept. Traditionally poets have been free to invoke place as a territory between

20. Eavan Boland, "Famine Roads," in *Irish Hunger: Personal Reflections on the Legacy of the Famine*, ed. Tom Hayden (Niwot, Colo.: Roberts Rinehart, 1997), 221.
21. Eavan Boland, *Object Lessons: The Life of the Woman and the Poet in our Time* (New York: W. W. Norton, 1996).
22. Ibid., 5.

invention and creation. I myself might once have proposed it as an act of imagination or an article of faith. But here, on a blue summer morning, I could feel it to be what it has been for so many: brute, choiceless fact.[23]

Boland, thus, needs to negotiate between the historically uninformed dailiness of her present suburban life and a place saturated with painful meaning, to which she is connected by her descent from the workhouse's superintendent. After the visit to Clonmel, she offers an aphorism that might be said to encapsulate the whole essay: "We yield to our present, but we choose our past."[24] Boland's choice of pasts finds her unwilling to speculate about her grandfather, who was complicit in furtherance of an inhumane system: "Standing there looking at the bleak length of the building, I refused to imagine him—my ancestor, with his shock of nut brown hair."[25] Unlike the anonymous women consigned to his care, such as it was, she notes that the physical record makes it possible to reclaim something of *his* life:

There was a small house with blunt gables and an outhouse. Was this where my great-grandfather lived? Where he stabled his pony, collected his ration, sheltered his children in the security of his position as overseer of other peoples' tragedies? At least, by these visible survivals, I could guess at his existence.[26]

But rather than look at the "knowable" record, Boland turns her genealogical gaze away from the retrievable facts of her great-grandfather's life and into the absences: the unrecorded history of an invented woman, of whom there is "no trace" of her existence. Boland's deliberately ahistorical method of recovering the past inserts an imagined woman into the picture. Like Boland herself, her proto-victim is in her thirties with two small children. Unlike Boland, the imagined woman (who is never identified as a relative, but is someone to whom Boland can feel connected, toward whom

23. Ibid., 162–63.   24. Ibid., 163.
25. Ibid.   26. Ibid., 164.

she can make an empathetic leap across generations) faces a fore-shortened life of suffering and "carefully planned monotony."[27] The essay limns the realities of a life in burgeoning suburbia lived under the aspect of this woman's silent suffering, who "cast her shadow cross the suburb."[28]

Chris Arthur is an Irish essayist who has also made forays into genealogy. Born in Belfast, and who worked formerly as a naturalist in Northern Ireland, Arthur has studied Buddhism and taught for many years in Wales. He appears to be making a bid to establish himself as Ireland's most energetic advocate of the creative nonfiction genre. He writes with a clear sense of his descent from such masterful forbears as Hubert Butler, and his meditative 1999 volume *Irish Nocturnes*[29] leads to comparisons with the essays of Annie Dillard—including, it must be admitted, points where he falls into Dillard's brand of easy universalizing. His writing on ancestry and descent falls into such a pattern; rather than seek the details of a vanished ancestor's life, as the other writers considered here have done, Arthur's writing on genealogy moves toward sweeping conclusions.

In his first collection, Arthur gathers essays that he calls "nocturnes," a term that consciously evokes the composer John Field's contemplative invention. One of the more autobiographical and most engaging nocturnes in the collection is titled "Facing the Family." In it, he takes up the question of his own genealogy.

The essay opens with Arthur being asked precisely the question that Michael Coady asked himself: "Do you know where your great-grandfather is buried?" In this case, the query is posed by a Japanese hereditary Temple Master who could trace his ancestry back through century after century. Arthur is compelled to admit that, no, he does not. But he has a number of artifacts that have come down to him from that great-grandfather or his generation that are

27. Ibid., 165.
28. Ibid., 171.
29. Chris Arthur, *Irish Nocturnes* (Aurora, Colo.: Davies Group, 1999).

charged with a sense of genealogical gravity. These include a plow forged at his Letterkenny blacksmith's shop and a linen carver on which many a meal was prepared. Arthur owns photographs that he knows show the faces of his great-grandparents, but, in a powerful statement of his own dissociation from his family history, he admits doesn't know who is who. Looking into these portraits, he writes,

Sometimes I think I see some ghostly continuity, a familial echo, as if two apparent islands separated by time's ocean were, in fact, connected underwater. More often though, the islands just seem like islands, tiny, isolated, separate, indistinguishable from the millions of others.[30]

Arthur also possesses the successive last wills and testaments of his family, including those of his great-grandfather—a possession that he describes in a luminous phrase as a "paper bog." He asks,

What would John Arthur have thought as "*Weak of body but of Sound Mind Memory & Judgment*" he made his X, that only three generations on, his descendants would have no idea where he had been "*decently interred*"? That the only trace of him on earth known to us, besides the deep, mute memory of generations, would be this single mark?[31]

Arthur's approach to his experience of a genealogical interruption runs exactly opposite to Coady's. Rather than strive to recover the particulars of his great-grandfather's life, he opts instead to locate himself in the cosmic anonymity of descent:

I can't help wondering, though, what the result would be if our contemporary sense of family—narrow, attenuated, limited to a couple of generations at most—were to be widened. Might this edge us closer to those all-inclusive senses of relationship that some religious ideas of love and compassion seem to strive for, a kind of universal kinship?[32]

30. Ibid., 182. 31. Ibid., 190.
32. Ibid., 194.

Flowering Absences

Arthur speaks of his fascination with "imaginary biography" in another nocturne titled "Invasions," his term for "little time-ambushes, when present consciousness is suddenly confronted with a piece of history dropped squarely in its path."[33] In "Facing the Family," he sidesteps these century-leaping "invasions" by responding with generalities. Compared to the rich imaginings of Coady and Boland, where imagination and biography truly do intersect, Arthur's work proves less intimate. By declining to conjecture about the missing ancestors, Arthur is more scrupulously factual than either Coady or Boland, but also leaves readers less satisfied; his genealogical inquiry fails to make a comparable emotional claim on the reader. One gets the feeling that the material is being forced and that the subject matter stands at a distance from the author. Perhaps a genealogical memoir that is not anchored in the particular is not really a memoir, at all—even if those particulars are, in the last analysis, fictional.

Unabashedly fictionalizing the past is exactly how the American poet Brendan Galvin deals with the gaps he encountered in his retrieval of his Irish origins. A native of Boston now living on Cape Cod, Galvin is a third-generation Irish American. He has been a frequent visitor to Ireland ever since his family insisted on taking him there for his first trip when he was in his forties. Irish themes percolate throughout his books. He has published a 1991 verse retelling of the Brendan legend, *Saints in Their Ox-Hide Boat*,[34] and in 1989 published a chapbook, *Raising Irish Walls*,[35] that collects a dozen or so of his most explicitly Irish poems. In his Irish poems, as in all his other work, Galvin pays scrupulous attention to nature and to landscape as he records "geophanies," to use Tim Robinson's term for those moments when the natural world seems to speak to us.[36]

Fragmentary family stories, passed down from previous gener-

33. Ibid., 93.
34. Brendan Galvin, *Saints in Their Ox-Hide Boat* (Baton Rouge: Louisiana State University Press, 1991).
35. Galvin, *Raising Irish Walls* (Bristol, R.I.: Ampersand, 1989).
36. Tim Robinson, "Listening to the Landscape," in *Setting Foot on the Shores of Connemara and Other Writings* (Dublin: Lilliput, 2007), 164.

ations, diffuse through these poems: for example, his grandmother's poaching, his family's work in the building trades in America. Yet a sense of the irretrievability of his family history recurs in his Irish poems. In "Himself," about his grandfather, he writes of looking into family photos:

> I hunt up the photo of Greenhorns
> that emptied me the first time
> I looked into the faces of steerage
>
> But he is the never-there,
> an absence even in these snapshots
> yellowed as though in some
> nicotine fit of time.[37]

In "Donegal," Galvin addresses his grandfather:

> The crossroads
> where I try to place you
> could be on Iceland
> or the moon, and all
> I hoard of you won't fill the
> the shallowest socket
> rain has worked in limestone
>
> Were you to stand under
> a signpost here, translating
> *An Clochán Liath* for me
> I wouldn't know you
> as I don't know what flowers
> ascetically out of these rocks.[38]

The Irish placename *An Clochán Liath* translates as "The Grey Rock" and is the defining feature of the local landscape in which Galvin feels a sense of removal and detachment. It is a landscape of story and association that Galvin, as an outsider, needs to have translated for him.

37. Galvin, *Raising Irish Walls*, 12.
38. Ibid., 24.

Flowering Absences

But Galvin makes a wholly imaginative response when confronted with a genealogical dead end: the option of simply making it up. He announces, and even boasts about, this approach in his poem "Inventing Ballygalvin."

His looking into the family tree does not start in a total vacuum. A relative in Massachusetts had done much of the genealogical legwork for him and had, in fact, tracked down the townland on the Inishowen peninsula from which the Galvin family emigrated. The poet wrote to him repeatedly before taking a trip to Ireland, but, for whatever reason, his cousin steadfastly declined to answer the letters. Knowing only that his father's family came from West Cork, and that his mother's family, the McLaughlins, came from Donegal and having no verifiable connection to any particular place in Ireland, Galvin decides instead to imagine one, and to make fresh the standard travel experiences that tens of thousands of travelers have encountered by assigning them a unique habitation in his own fanciful place of origin:

> Because my cousin the priest
> knows but won't tell me
> where the family's from, I've invented
> this West Cork townland. I admire
> its sheepdogs' individual styles
> as one has at my car head-on
> and another snipes from wayside fuchsia.[39]

The inexplicably close-mouthed relative who "knows but won't tell" is a frequently encountered figure in genealogical anecdotes; in fact, the poem gleefully collects and serves up stereotypical Irish experience. "Inventing Ballygalvin" presents scenes that might be lifted off any postcard rack in Ireland: crumbling castles, stone bridges, sheep moving like "walking topiary." He excludes the priest cousin and his ilk from Ballygalvin:

39. Ibid., 20–21.

> There's no pink hotel here
> for golfing monsignors in green hats,
> only this bog of moor grass and black rush,
> which lubbers onto the road
> full of years of rain.

Another stereotypical experience that Galvin has in Ireland is that of the doppelgänger—the finite number of Irish physiognomic types leading to the inevitable meetings with someone who looks just like someone else. In "Ballygalvin," he writes, "I'll have to watch / I don't meet myself rounding a corner"; or as his fictitious cousin (who fills potholes for an equally fictitious county board) says,

> Turns out that faces in Ireland
> are faces in Boston,
> somebody's rotating
> the living and the dead.[40]

At one level, "Inventing Ballygalvin" may be merely a playful, even impish, poem. At another level, though, it may be suggesting something important to our understanding of how genealogy can inform creative literature. Galvin's locating of the imagination as a viable homeland for genealogy merits our attention. He effectively reverses the conventional graveyard meditation and stands it on its head: rather than settle for a blurry sense of connection to the anonymous generations that have gone before him, Galvin takes universal, even generic, Irish moments and creates out of them a highly particular place and time.

In doing so, he adds to the growing body of creative literature spurred by genealogical concerns—a literature that, at its best, conveys a generosity of spirit; that turns away from egotism and self-certainty in order to embrace incertitude and disruption as the source of art; and that enriches our understandings of both the past and present by making informed leaps of imagination.

---

40. Ibid., 22.

7

'Tis, Meaning *Maybe*

The Uncertain Last Words of *Angela's Ashes*

Frank McCourt's *Angela's Ashes: A Memoir* has been attended by varying degrees of controversy since its publication in 1996.[1] The most
vigorous of these debates have been over questions of accuracy,
including charges that the book is so willfully falsified that it is
not a memoir at all.[2] Little debate, however, has centered on the
enigmatic precise last word of the book—the single word *'Tis* that
comprises the entire last chapter—spoken at the time of the narrator's arrival in the United States. Given the fixation on leaving Ireland that pervades the book up until this point, it is unsurprising
that the ending has been almost universally read as affirming. A

An earlier version of this chapter appeared under the same title in *Études Irlan-
daises* 36, no. 2 (Autumn 2011), and is reprinted with permission.
   1. Frank McCourt, *Angela's Ashes: A Memoir* (New York: Scribner's, 1996).
   2. See, for instance, Margaret O'Brien Steinfels, "I Knew Angela, Did Frank
McCourt?" *Commonweal* 124, no. 7 (November 7, 1997): 7, in which Steinfels disputes
essential facts in McCourt's presentation of his mother. The dispute over McCourt's
accuracy and/or inaccuracy was especially vigorous in Limerick City; see, for instance, Warren Hoge, "Limerick, Burned, Also Finds a Salve in 'Angela's Ashes,'"
New York Times, August 31, 1997.

reviewer in *Salon,* for instance, summed up the opinion of many when he referred to Frank's emigration as an escape for the "hell" of Limerick[3] and the arrival in America and "his most triumphant moment." The narrator often speaks of America as a place of deliverance; not long before his departure, while still in Limerick, he writes in desperation that "if I can't get to America I might as well jump into the River Shannon."[4] Yet, his first hours in America—despite its construction, in his mind, as an escape from an intolerable captivity—do not seem to be attended by any great sense of relief, nor does our reading of the final page provide what Frank Kermode famously termed "the sense of an ending."[5] If we look more closely at the exchange that concludes the memoir, there is reason to believe that the book's ending is more open-ended than is generally recognized; in fact, the closing word, *'Tis,* might more accurately be said to bespeak a deep ambivalence toward the goal of taking up a new life in America that Frank has held before him throughout most of his childhood and adolescence in Ireland.

Following the blockbuster success of the memoir, the suddenly famous McCourt gleefully assumed a public persona that was to all purposes that of the media's default Irishman, for which his Irish brogue and, yes, blarney, was an inevitable accoutrement. There is a fair amount of blarney in the memoir, too, and McCourt writes of his arrival in the New World in conspicuously Irish cadences. In brief, the book concludes when, after Frank and Tim Boyle (a shipboard acquaintance) have an unexpected sexual encounter with two women whom they meet on their first night in the New World, Boyle says, "My God, that was a lovely night, Frank."[6] At that point,

3. In this chapter, I will refer to the narrator of the book as Frank; when the discussion centers on the author's narrative strategies and choices, I will refer to McCourt.

4. McCourt, *Angela's Ashes,* 300.

5. Frank Kermode, *The Sense of an Ending: Studies in the Theory of Fiction* (New York: Oxford University Press, 1967).

6. Following Joyce, McCourt never uses quotation marks when presenting dialogue; however, they have occasionally been introduced in this chapter for purposes of clarity. Note, too, that in this statement the capital *G* on the word "God" is not

chapter 18 ends with Boyle asking, or rather, asserting, "Isn't this a great country altogether?" The reader turns the page to find a single word as chapter 19: '*Tis*.[7]

It is only appropriate that *Angela's Ashes* end with spoken dialogue. At its best, the book's highly oral and anecdotal quality, honed in its origins as a two-hander stage piece, serves to carry along what can be an excruciating tale. Those are also qualities that grate on many readers. One of the more persistent criticisms of *Angela's Ashes* is its sheer volubility: even one of the book's outspoken admirers, Edward A. Hagan, concedes that the book is "riddled with repetitiveness."[8] John Henry Raleigh's arch comment that mere loquacity, and not eloquence, is the real gift of the Irish—"the motto of the Irish, especially the drinking Irish, is that a thing is not said until it is repeated almost ad infinitum"[9]—might be said to be apotheosized by *Angela's Ashes*.

But it does not end that way. A book that has specialized in logorrhea ends in a one-word chapter. How are we to understand the puzzling authorial decision to end a long-winded book with a monosyllabic final chapter?

Proving or disproving the accuracy of McCourt's account of the Limerick slums is not the purview of this chapter.[10] However, it may be pertinent to note that this enigmatic ending follows on a sequence of events that give even a sympathetic reader reason

---

an accident; it signals that, notwithstanding his claims to the contrary, McCourt remains steeped in Catholicism and, despite his rejection of the watchful priest's morality, at an unconscious level he is still observing its pieties.

7. McCourt, *Angela's Ashes*, 363–64.

8. Edward A. Hagan, "Really an Alley Cat?: *Angela's Ashes* and Critical Orthodoxy," *New Hibernia Review* 4, no. 4 (Winter 2000): 41.

9. John Henry Raleigh, "O'Neill's *Long Day's Journey into Night* and New England Irish-Catholicism," in *O'Neill: A Collection of Critical Essays*, ed. John Gassner (Englewood Cliffs, N.J.: Prentice-Hall, 1964), 130.

10. For the record, I believe there is ample reason to doubt the veracity of many elements in *Angela's Ashes*, especially in its later portions. However, I also believe McCourt's portrayal of Irish urban poverty in *Angela's Ashes* is generally accurate. The McCourts were not merely poor; they were exceptionally poor, even in comparison to their already deprived neighbors.

to doubt McCourt's narrative reliability. The providential details of how he gets what he terms his "escape money"[11]—and "escape" is not too strong a word—involving a much-too-convenient death and an attendant windfall, strain plausibility. Frank sails to New York on the *Irish Oak*. On board, a watchful priest befriends him; accompanied by the priest, on their first night in the United States as he and Tim Boyle stumble into their sexual encounter with the brassy American women, the encounter happens with the priest sitting just outside the door: in fact he knocks on the door while Frank and "Freda" are in the midst of having sex. At that moment, Frank—speaking in the book's insistent present tense—says he does not "give a fiddler's fart if the Pope himself knocked at the door and the College of Cardinals gathered gawking at the window."[12] It is clearly a little too good to be true that the priest is waiting outside the door and a little too obvious that the woman's name would be Freda, as in "freedom"; the episode with Freda resonates with the spurious letters columns of men's magazines.

But whatever the facts, this is how it does end, and presumably, it is how McCourt wants us to understand his arrival in America. To understand this sudden brevity, it is helpful to remember that, in Irish usage, the expression *'Tis* almost always takes its meaning from the question or statement that preceded it—in this case, "Isn't this a great country altogether?"

As noted, Frank's attitude toward America is generally presumed to be highly positive. As a boy, the images that come to him through motion pictures powerfully shape his understanding of America. His film-inflected fantasy of America is largely a matter of cowboy and gangster movies, but it is also a place that represents an emotional freedom, as in the poignant comment at a rare moment of affection toward his alcoholic father; "if I were in America I could say, I love you Dad the way they do in the films but you can't do that in Limerick for fear you might be laughed at."[13]

11. McCourt, *Angela's Ashes*, 334.   12. Ibid., 362.
13. Ibid., 201.

'Tis, Meaning *Maybe*

One strain of commentary on *Angela's Ashes* holds that the author's motivations were both cynical and manipulative, driven by what he believed would appeal to the American market, starting with the first words of the book: "My father and mother should have stayed in New York."[14] The closing exchange between Frank and Tim Boyle is conspicuously near to the brogue of Stage Irishry; here and elsewhere, McCourt walks close to babuism. Not only does McCourt wheel out tired old stereotypes, his detractors say; he also panders to American self-satisfaction. In this interpretation, after three hundred pages of telling Irish Americans what they wanted to hear about Old World pig-in-the parlor Irish irresponsibility and filth, McCourt then reminds Americans how much better, and better off, they are than the Irish. Nowhere was this more scathingly asserted than in Roy Foster's 1999 review, "'Tisn't: The Million-Dollar Blarney of the McCourts," in the *New Republic*. Foster charges *Angela's Ashes* with toadying to "the complex attitude of the United States to what it expects the Irish to be, and the enduring pride and reassurance that Americans find in hot water and flush lavatories."[15] At a minimum, most commentators on *Angela's Ashes* assert that the closing chapter represents an embrace of America. James B. Mitchell, for instance, writes that "McCourt argues, on the page and in person, for the achievability of the American Dream."[16] George O'Brien's fine essay "The Last Word: Reflections on *Angela's Ashes*," in *New Perspectives on the Irish Diaspora* (2000), speaks of McCourt "making the *concluding* and *conclusive* affirmation of 'Tis, referring to how great a country America is."[17]

14. Ibid., 11. McCourt may indeed betray a certain cynicism—though he describes it as inventive pedagogy—when in *Teacher Man* (New York: Scribner's, 2005), his memoir of his years as a New York secondary schoolteacher, he quite unabashedly admits that he related and embellished stories of his Irish childhood in order to keep his students quiet.

15. Roy Foster, "'Tisn't: The Million-Dollar Blarney of the McCourts," *New Republic*, November 1, 1999.

16. James B. Mitchell, "Popular Autobiography as Historiography: The Reality Effect of *Angela's Ashes*," *Biography* 26, no. 4 (2003): 621.

17. George O'Brien, "The Last Word: Reflections on *Angela's Ashes*," in *New Per-*

Yet, when an Irish person speaks the word '*Tis,* the statement should by no means be understood as certain. Often, in Irish conversation, '*Tis* is precisely a way of saying nothing, of merely keeping the conversation going, like a nod, "go on," or "uh-huh." It is hard to understand how George O'Brien, a native of Wexford, would call the word "conclusive": he surely has heard such an utterance used to convey a full range of meanings, at least some of which are tepid—closer to "So it seems" or "Yes, I guess so" than to any ringing affirmation. (There is, of course, an Irish classic that *does* end with a ringing affirmation: Molly Bloom's "yes I will Yes" at the end of *Ulysses,* which, for that matter, is also a book that ends with a homecoming.[18] The affirmation of Molly's *Yes* is beyond dispute; McCourt's '*Tis* is a far less enthusiastic utterance.)

The likelihood that the closing word is neither concluding not conclusive, but rather a remark that leans toward the tentative, is underscored by the author's deliberate hesitation. McCourt, in effect, takes a breath—and requires his readers to take a breath—before the final word. He pauses; he needs to think about the question Tim Boyle has just put.

Notably, the exchange occurs almost literally between two worlds, after Frank's first night in the New World. The abandon of Frank's encounter with Freda notwithstanding, recklessness—sexual or otherwise—is not the norm for newly landed immigrants. In reality, new immigrants proceed cautiously. In *Angela's Ashes,* that caution displays itself in both the moderation of the final word and, more important, in the consciously inserted pause, the space between chapters. The hesitation anticipates America's grudging embrace, if it is an embrace, of the new arrival.[19] The pause bears

---

spectives on the Irish Diaspora, ed. Charles Fanning (Carbondale, Ill.: Southern Illinois University Press, 2000), 236; emphasis added.

18. James Joyce, *Ulysses,* ed. Hans Walter Gabler (New York: Random House, 1986), 608.

19. The playing-out of the immigrant's arrival is told in McCourt's second volume of memoir, entitled '*Tis: A Memoir* (New York: Scribner's, 1999). Although the second book almost universally disappointed readers, its generally hopeful tone

witness to the inescapable liminality of Irish-American identity and immigrant identity more generally—the often superficial but occasionally profound experience of being both on the inside and on the outside in two different places. An ambiguous identity has always followed the immigrant in the New World, who is categorized by others as Irish while in America and American when back in Ireland; Frank feels this with special acuity with regard to his accent, which is mocked as foreign in both countries. His immigrant dividedness is at least doubled, in this instance, by the fact that this is a re-immigration.

Although more than 90 percent of the book takes place in Ireland, *Angela's Ashes* is in fact an Irish-American story, told by a United States citizen who was born in New York and had been a resident of the United States for nearly fifty years at the time of publication. Notably, it is also a book that begins and ends in America. When Tim Boyle asks Frank to assess America, it is not on his moment of arrival but on his moment of return. The narrator has been here before: he knows this "great country altogether" is where a brother died and a place so awful for his parents that, incredibly, they preferred to return to Ireland.

Among the most familiar patterns of autobiography is that of introducing a point of origin, followed by a period in which the autobiographer rejects, or at least moves away from, the point of departure before a concluding return in which the point of origin or source is seen with a new insight and maturity.[20] As it is a story of re-immigration, this pattern applies tidily to *Angela's Ashes.* Frank's last glimpse of the place that he is now being asked to endorse as "a great country" took this form:

The ship pulled away from the dock. Mam said, That's the Statue of Liberty and Ellis Island where all the immigrants came in. Then she

---

suggests that in the sequel, the single word does affirm without ambiguity. It might also suggest that the matter was unresolved at the close of the first book.

20. The pattern is compellingly examined with reference to religious life writing in David Leigh, *Circuitous Journeys: Modern Spiritual Autobiography* (New York: Fordham University Press, 2000).

leaned over the side and vomited and the wind from the Atlantic blew it all over us and other happy people admiring the view. Passengers cursed and ran, seagulls came from all over the harbor, and Mam hung limp and pale on the ship's rail.[21]

This is scarcely a memory that would prepare McCourt for a joyous return.

Having the final chapter comprise only a single word puts a great deal of weight on that word. It might be helpful, then, to look elsewhere in the book to how the word is used when it appears as the last word in a conversational exchange. The phrase crops up less often than might be expected, though we do encounter it from time to time embedded in sentences and phrases like "'Tis a sad day for Ireland" and so on. However, there are only four instances, before the end of *Angela's Ashes*, in which the word '*Tis* appears as a freestanding or nearly freestanding sentence. None occurs in an emotionally neutral context.

The word '*Tis* first appears when the family is in the North of Ireland, and, unable to find work or charity there, they determine to relocate to the Free State where they have a better chance of getting on the dole. Looking out at Lough Neagh, the father weaves a story about how someday they will return there to swim, and to eat fried eels as Cuchulain once ate them raw "because there's great power in an eel." Frank then asks,

Is that right, dad?
'Tis.[22]

By this point, we as readers understand that Frank is being duped; we know, but Frank does not, that when his father says '*Tis* here, there is no reason to believe him; the father's fecklessness will assure that they never return to this poignant scene.

The next time we hear the word '*Tis* occurs seventy pages later, again from his father, and again accompanied by a reference to

21. McCourt, *Angela's Ashes*, 46.
22. Ibid., 51.

Ireland of the sagas. There, the young Frankie is preparing for his First Communion when another child tells him a "dirty story" about how Emer became Cuchulain's wife and how the women assembled on the plains of Muirthemne and had a "pissing contest."[23] Frank is tormented by religious scruples about whether he needs to confess this and, in an admittedly maudlin passage, has a child's mystical experience when he hears the Angel on the Seventh Step say "be not afraid" and instructs him to go ahead and confess it. Notably—given the later encounter with Freda—the "angel" in question is associated with sexual innocence and/or ignorance. The "Angel on the Seventh Step" is the McCourt family's coded version of the stork story, their chaste explanation of where babies come from. In any case, Frankie confides both his scruples and his vision to his father, who—in a rare moment of sobriety and availability—tells him not to worry:

> All right. Tell the priest if you like but the Angel on the Seventh Step said that only because you didn't tell me first. Isn't it better to tell your father your troubles than an angel who is a light and a voice in your head?
> 'Tis, Dad.[24]

But, again, we know that when the trusting word *'Tis* is spoken here, it is a prelude to disappointment: the father will only sporadically and unpredictably be available for his son before eventually abandoning the family.

The next time we encounter the word in this way, it is associated with McCourt's mother Angela, and again touches on an element of religious scruples. She and a group of women are enjoying a cigarette together; Angela complains that her husband cannot control himself, either sexually or with regard to drink, like other men can.[25] (This and other such scenes give rise to one of the most frequently voiced challenges to McCourt's narrative reliability: that

---

23. Ibid., 123.   24. Ibid., 125.

25. For a thoughtful consideration of the multiple narrative strategies at work in *Angela's Ashes*, see Shannon Forbes, "Performative Identity Formation in Frank McCourt's *Angela's Ashes: A Memoir*," *Journal of Narrative Theory* 37, no. 3 (2007): 473–96.

he reports on conversations that he would have had no way of knowing, including conversations that took place before he was born.) Angela's worries over the family's financial straits lead her to sigh, "I don't know under God what I'm going to do." Then,

Bridey drags on her Woodbine, drinks her tea and declares that God is good. Mam says she's sure God is good for someone somewhere but He hasn't been seen lately on the lanes of Limerick.

Bridey laughs, Oh, Angela, you could go to hell for that, and Mam says, Aren't I there already Bridey?

And they laugh and drink their tea and smoke their Woodbines and tell one another that the fag is the only comfort they have.

'Tis.[26]

We encounter the word *'Tis* multiple times—so often that McCourt appears to be deliberately calling attention to it—in a scene that occurs just after an incident when Frank, who has regularly skipped his Irish dance classes and gone to the movies instead, is unexpectedly called on at the home of friend Paddy Clohessy to perform a traditional dance. Unable to take part in this emblematically Irish activity, he tries to fake it with an improvised hodgepodge about "The Walls of Limerick falling down . . . And the River Shannon kills us."[27] At that point, Angela comes to look for young Frank, where—rather than being angry at her son for skipping classes, she is consumed with sadness when she discovers that his friend's father is in fact an old sweetheart, Dennis Clohessy. Their exchange is shot through with recognition of their present unhappiness and remorse for choices made. McCourt shamelessly milks the pathos, to the point of having the elder Clohessy ask Angela to sing the sentimental lyrics, *"Oh the days of the Kerry Dancing . . . gone alas like our youth, too soon."*[28]

Here, and nowhere else in the book, we encounter the word repeatedly, though not always as the last word of a conversational ex-

---

26. McCourt, *Angela's Ashes*, 145–46.   27. Ibid., 165.
28. Ibid., 168.

change. In the three pages given over to this regret-filled moment, the word appears seven times, as in,

> God above, is that Angela?
> 'Tis, Mr Clohessy.

And in such small exchanges as

> He says 'Tis me, Dennis Clohessy, Angela.
> Ah, no.
> 'Tis, Angela.[29]

Mrs Clohessy says of her invalid husband, "'Tis his own fault for not going in the hospital, so'tis."[30] Clohessy asks, "Is America a dry place?" and is answered, *'Tis.*[31] And as they walk home, Angela weeps. One of the children tries to comfort her, assuring his mother that Frankie will not run away again, at which point Angela "lifts him and hugs him and says, Oh, no, Michael, 'tisn't Frankie I'm crying about. 'Tis Dennis Clohessy and the dancing nights at the Wembley Hall and the fish and chips after."[32]

McCourt, thus, prepares for the closing *'Tis* of chapter 19 by earlier calling attention to the word in scenes that are freighted with remorse, with future disappointment, and with religious scruples. All of these elements attend McCourt's reply in the closing answer.

The religious scruples are of particular relevance. McCourt reacts to the events upon his arrival neither with relief nor with an unmixed delight in his sudden sexual freedom. Nothing in *Angela's Ashes* suggests that he would be blasé about the peril to his soul in such an illicit encounter; he remains in all ways an Irish Catholic. His adolescence in Ireland was wracked by guilt over his sexual encounter with the tubercular Theresa—guilt that was only relieved for him by going to Confession. But here again, ambiguity characterizes McCourt's tale. *Angela's Ashes* most assuredly attacks the hypocrisy of the Catholic Church in Ireland, and Angela bitterly denounces the priests who slammed the door in her son's face. But

29. Ibid., 167.   30. Ibid., 168.
31. Ibid.   32. Ibid., 169.

it is also the case that virtually the only shred of comfort he ever finds in Ireland comes from the priest to whom he unburdens himself in the Franciscan church. On his return to the New World, the priest who knocks at the door while Frank is having sex provides a powerful reminder that (except for the moment of sexual climax itself) the moral strictures and certainties of his youth have not been disabled.

Frank's profound uneasiness about being watched by God, by the priests, and by the continuations of the restricting social norms that governed his earlier life in Ireland lend themselves readily to Foucault's theorizing of social control by means of the Panopticon. In *Discipline and Punish*, Foucault proposes that the structures of modern social control in effect replicate the model prison designed by Jeremy Bentham in 1785; that is, the all-seeing eye that not only regulates behavior but also implicates the confined in their own scrutiny, "caught up in a power situation on which they themselves are the bearers."[33] In doing so, Panopticon provides an inverted form of comfort.

McCourt's coming to America was possible only because he was momentarily able to escape the Panopticon of Limerick, where, as in Bentham's model, "the gaze is alert everywhere."[34] Young Frank had a secret job writing threatening letters for the usurer Mrs. Finucane. One day, he arrives at her house to find her dead of a heart attack, with her unlocked strongbox in her lap. The money pays for his passage, but Frank is not the only one released; he also seizes and destroys her ledger of money lent, thereby anonymously freeing much of Limerick from crushing debt. A little too Dickensian to be believed, but McCourt asks us to believe it.

But one does not leave a prison easily; an essential point of Foucault's theorizing of panoptic structures is that they become internalized. Even without the priest waiting in the ante-room—who has

33. Michel Foucault, *Discipline and Punish: The Birth of the Prison*, trans. Alan Sheridan (New York: Vintage, 1999), 201.
34. Ibid., 195.

already warned him, "These are bad women. We won't stay here long"[35]—Frank, having assumed the self-disciplining that is the goal of Panopticon, could not be unconflicted in these circumstances. And indeed they do not stay there long; the liaison with Freda is very much a "quickie," but is long enough for Frank to surrender completely to the sexual encounter. As Foucault notes, engaging in alternative sexualities—or, perhaps, for young man raised in the moral strictures of mid-twentieth-century Ireland, engaging in sexuality, period—is one of the ways we resist or defy the Panopticon. McCourt specifically points to this response in his remark that he would not care if the pope himself were watching.

Notably, such resistance obtains only in those moments of defiance: the containing power of the Panopticon's watchfulness remains. McCourt never asks us to believe he has broken out of the old morality; Frank leaves with the priest, flushed with embarrassment, in a tailspin of worry about what his mother would think and much else.

The last word of the book answers a question; Frank also enters the book by being asked a question. The opening pages of *Angela's Ashes* provide the background to his transient early childhood. Frank himself does not enter *Angela's Ashes* until page 19, when, on a Brooklyn playground, his brother Malachy has some sort of an accident on a see-saw. Angela, at this point his very pregnant mother, runs over and

> She says, What did you do? What did you do to the child?
> I don't know what to say. I don't know what I did.[36]

In other words, when we meet Frank he is three years old and does not know what to say; when we leave him at the other end of the book, he is nineteen years old, and he is still unsure how to answer a question. And, in fact, his unarticulated but unquestionably present scruples about his encounter with the sex-crazed American

35. McCourt, *Angela's Ashes*, 361.
36. Ibid., 19.

woman might be phrased in similar words: What did you do? What did you do to the child—that is, to the child you were back in Ireland?

Questions, of course, play a central role in any memoir or fictionalized treatment of childhood; it is in asking questions that the narrators of such memoirs register their evolving consciousness and self-awareness and their entry into the generally confused and uncertain world of adulthood. The complicating factor in Frank's childhood is that his Ireland is a place seemingly bereft of adult uncertainty. In the Limerick of McCourt's youth, no male adult—and very few women—will admit to a tincture of doubt about anything. Their confident pronouncements mask an underlying cluelessness, of course. His father from the North of Ireland has no idea how to break into the networks of Limerick; the priests have no idea how to deal with the problems of the poor; the civil authorities have no idea how to manage the country (and so leave those matters to those same bumbling priests); and the schoolteachers are variously ignorant, obsessively rule-bound, and abusive.

Angela's Ashes abounds with instances in which adults provide unsatisfying, but authoritative, answers. Early on, Frank and Malachy are walking with their father in the countryside, leading to this exchange: "What are cows dad? Cows are cows, son." More questions from the child follow until "My father barked at him, Is there any end to your questions? Sheep are sheep, cows are cows, and that over there is a goat. A goat is a goat."[37] Later, a simple-minded neighbor known as The Abbott offers the tautology that "Apples is apples and bread is bread."[38]

Frank's classrooms are likewise places where questions lead only to unwarranted certainty or to abuse, never to an answer that is useful or informative. Religious instruction in particular takes the form of rote learning. For instance, Mr. Benson, the master charged with preparing Frank and his classmates to receive their First Com-

37. Ibid., 47.
38. Ibid., 301.

munion, tells the class that it is his goal "to beat the idler out of us and the Sanctifying Grace into us."[39] The master goes into a tirade when a boy asks what Sanctifying Grace is; the master dismisses the very idea that a young person might display curiosity or interrogate the received answers:

You're here to learn the catechism and to do what you're told. You're not here to be asking questions. There are too many people wandering the world and that's what has us in the state we're in and if I find any boy in this class asking questions I won't be responsible for what happens.[40]

When a classmate forgets himself and asks another question, the master flies into a rage. Benson thunders that if another boy asks a question, he will

> flog that boy until the blood spurts.
> What will I do boys?
> Flog the boy, sir.
> Till?
> Till the blood spurts, sir.[41]

In every classroom, not just those devoted to religious instruction, the pedagogy is always that of the catechism, in which the student is expected to parrot apodictic truths. Children, in McCourt's Limerick, are assumed to be little adults: they are expected both to know everything already and to agree with what they are told.[42]

In this authoritarian environment, adult certainty, even when it is wildly mistaken, rules over all. There are only expected answers befitting proscribed roles. In no instance, in the whole of

39. Ibid., 118. 40. Ibid.
41. Ibid., 119.

42. The social marginality of Irish children has been examined in detail in a number of recent studies, including Joseph Dunne and James Kelly, eds., *Childhood and Its Discontents: The First Seamus Heaney Lectures* (Dublin: Liffey Press, 2002); John Countryman and Kelly Matthews, eds., *The Country of the Young: Interpretations of Youth and Childhood in Irish Culture* (Dublin: Four Courts, 2013); and Maria Luddy and James Smith, eds., *Children, Childhood and Irish Society, 1500 to the Present* (Dublin: Four Courts, 2014).

Frank's young life—except perhaps during the illicit literary discussions he has during his hospitalizations, discussions that violate an imposed rule of silence—is Frank ever asked a question that legitimately seeks an answer. Children like Frank, having been battered into silence and submission, find no room for self-awareness to develop. As James B. Mitchell notes, "One of the conceits of *Angela's Ashes* is that the 'I' seems to have been formed externally, as if McCourt's subjectivity developed only through interacting with others, rather than developed in concert with introspective reflection."[43] In the Ireland of *Angela's Ashes*, questions get asked only for the purpose of soliciting agreement.

Thus, when his fellow emigrant Tim Boyle asks, "Isn't this a great country altogether?" he surely expects no ambiguity. The expected answer would be for Frank to look him in the eye and assert, Yes, absolutely. But that is not the answer Frank gives: he responds with hesitation. Edward Hagan is correct about the meaning of McCourt's final *'Tis* when he writes that it "represents a consciousness evolving from the certainty of patriarchal assertion, to the ambiguity of Frank's 'midatlantic' situation."[44] McCourt's last word assents to, but does not embrace, the prior question.

Tim Boyle may think that arrival in America was an occasion for the fireworks of a sudden sexual liberty. But that is not the only freedom conferred upon Frank McCourt. On his first night back in the New World, he has also been given the freedom to think about his answer. In the understated last word, we see that Frank's voyage has, at last, brought him to a place where he has the liberty to speak from interiority and reflection.

43. Mitchell, "Popular Autobiography as Historiography," 612.
44. Hagan, "Really an Alley Cat?," 42.

8

"Someone Watching Your Back"

Guardian Angels in Michael Patrick MacDonald's *All Souls*

The arrest of the notorious South Boston gangster James "Whitey" Bulger in June 2011 brought renewed attention to one of the most compelling memoirs of recent American history, Michael Patrick MacDonald's *All Souls: A Family Story from Southie* (1999).[1] MacDonald— a community activist who came to prominence for having established the gun buy-back programs in Boston—recounts a violence-filled childhood in the conspicuously Irish Catholic neighborhood of "Southie," or South Boston. His story opens during the busing crisis of the 1970s that brought federal troops to the street and continues through the author's coming of age in the 1980s in the midst of a crack cocaine epidemic.

An earlier version of this chapter was originally published under the same title in *American Catholic Studies* 123, no. 1 (Spring 2012), and is reprinted here with permission.

1. Michael Patrick MacDonald, *All Souls: A Family Story from Southie* (New York: Ballantine, 1999). The arrest of Bulger was a national and international news story; see, for example, Adam Nagourney and Ian Lovett, "Whitey Bulger Is Arrested in California," *New York Times*, June 23, 2011. MacDonald was frequently sought by

Religion is present throughout MacDonald's memoir, although the institutional church is detached from the terrifying events on the streets of Boston and, in the author's blunt assessment, largely irrelevant to the lives of his neighbors. But at the level of imagination and imagery—starting with a title that invokes the Communion of Saints—a Catholic vocabulary and sensibility is inescapable in the book. MacDonald himself has said that he "can't help but be very Catholic." Although he generally shies away from speaking of his spiritual life, in interviews and in public forums he has nonetheless articulated a clear sense of Christianity as a force that demands social activism, as in the tradition of Dorothy Day. "I love Catholicism, despite the problems I have with the church," he has said, adding that "I choose to work with its symbols and images in all of my life."[2] One of those images is the Guardian Angel.

Portrayed by the media as a tightly knit working-class neighborhood, a self-image reinforced by the local *South Boston Tribune* that regularly publishes "Our Beautiful World" features of church bazaars, first communions, and cake sales, the Southie of MacDonald's *All Souls* is a community in massive denial of its own misery. Against vast evidence to the contrary—including the deaths of hundreds of their children and neighbors—the people of Southie cling to the illusion that they live in a benign and self-regulating community. They also believe that they have for all purposes been misunderstood and abandoned by the larger community of Boston, the police, the courts, the media, the education system, and all of the institutions of civil society. MacDonald's account leaves little doubt that the latter assessment is in most ways true; though it is also true that there is a large measure of self-isolation at work, enforced by the nearly universal acceptance of the claim that "Southie takes care of its own."

Thus, a sort of siege mentality takes hold in the neighborhood:

---

media outlets to comment on the arrest; his publisher, Beacon Press, provides a listing of interviews and news articles at http://www.beacon.org/productdetails. cfm?PC=1877.

2. "A Conversation with Michael Patrick MacDonald," in "Reader's Guide," an appendix without page numbers following MacDonald, *All Souls*, 266.

"Someone Watching Your Back"

"It was us against them," MacDonald recalls, "as the neighborhood closed off more and more to the outside world."[3] Whether it admits it or not, Southie is keenly aware of its own powerlessness. In one memorable passage, MacDonald as a child stares long and hard at a saucer filled with drowned cockroaches and finds himself wondering, in words clearly meant to apply to his family and friends, "if they just didn't know they had wings, or if they had forgotten they had them until it was too late to save themselves."[4] Perhaps because of their isolation and sense of defenselessness, the people of Southie also prove uniquely attracted to the idea of having a special protector. One powerful, distinctly Catholic, and recurring image that informs *All Souls* is the trope of the Guardian Angel. Though the nature of those "angels" takes widely varying forms, the notion percolates throughout the memoir, both within the MacDonald family itself and for the neighborhood in a series of hoped-for defenders.

These supposed defenders include opportunistic politicians; anti-busing rioters who keep black students out of the high school and who figure the police as enemies; and most tragic of all, the unlikely person of Whitey Bulger—one of the most ruthless criminals in American history. And yet, as MacDonald writes,

No one made us feel better about where we lived than Whitey Bulger. Whitey was the brother of our own Senator Billy Bulger, but on the streets of Southie he was even more powerful than Billy. He was the king of Southie, but not like the bad English kings who oppressed and killed the poor people of Ireland. No way we would have put up with that. He had definite rules that we all learned to live by, not because we had to but because we wanted to. And we had to have someone looking out for us, with the likes of Judge Garrity [the judge who had ordered forced busing] trying to take away what little we'd gotten for ourselves.[5]

MacDonald's Southie continually struggles to overcome the cognitive dissonance contained between illusion and the reality of the

3. MacDonald, *All Souls*, 78. 4. Ibid., 72.
5. Ibid., 110.

neighborhood. The unadmitted Southie of this book is what the author, borrowing a term from the college sociology classes that he would later take, comes to realize is a "death zone." A full 85 percent of the families are on welfare; drugs and violence are pandemic; and a code of silence allows suicides, punishment beatings, and murders to go unremarked. There is probably no more affecting detail in this often brutal book than the incident when, as a child on the way to St. Augustine's Grade School, the author finds three amputated fingers on the sidewalk, and "It was nothing really—just another story to tell the kids at school."[6]

The family that faces this nightmare is headed by the author's mother, Helen King, or "Ma," the daughter of Irish immigrants who, like everything and everyone else in the skewed world of MacDonald's Southie, occupies a world of extremes: a highly sexualized single mother on welfare with a great devotion to the Virgin Mary and who indeed invites comparisons to the Pietà.

Reviewers of *All Souls* have almost inevitably been drawn to compare it to Frank McCourt's *Angela's Ashes* (1996). MacDonald's family can, in fact, go toe-to-toe with the McCourts of Limerick in tragedy, if not necessarily in day-to-day misery—for it has to be admitted that unlike the dreariness and exhaustion of *Angela's Ashes*, in *All Souls* there is (at least until the crack epidemic hits) a vigor and a strange sort of joy about life on the streets. The astonishing line-up of smiling Irish-looking children on the cover of both the hardcover and paperback version of the book hardly suggests the trauma that attends the family from page 1 forward. MacDonald was the seventh of Helen King's eleven children by several fathers. His mother lost one child to natural causes in infancy. Another son developed a psychosis, started electroshock therapy at age four, and finally committed suicide by throwing himself off a rooftop. A daughter endures permanent brain damage from a drug-induced fall off a roof (this daughter later becomes a cocaine addict and tries to sell her child, Fatima Marie, for $50). One son, her favorite,

6. Ibid., 136.

is murdered by his comrades in a botched bank robbery; another son starts dealing drugs at age nine and eventually hangs himself in prison. Later, one of the younger boys is imprisoned for a year for a killing he witnessed but did not commit. Similar stories could be replicated by all of MacDonald's neighbors in the Old Colony housing project; the story opens and closes at a vigil in a Catholic church at which the survivors of more than two hundred young people light candles in memory of their children and siblings lost to violence and drugs.

These passages, in which the physically and psychically wounded survivors of poverty, drugs, and gangster-sponsored attrition murders at last stand and admit their loss, are tremendously moving. Neighbor after neighbor comes forward and for the first time makes a statement of personal loss, finally breaking the enforced silences that forbade a proper grief.

MacDonald indicts the institutional church's disconnection from life on the streets when he describes the All Souls Day assembly in one of Southie's Catholic churches. After the father of a boy named P.J. (who died of a heroin overdose at fifteen) speaks, Mac-Donald writes:

The teenage boys looked down. I don't know if they cried: their Fightin' Irish baseball caps were pulled low to cast dark shadows on their eyes. There was a time when people would've told the kids to take off their baseball caps in church, but it was too late to teach the symbolic importance of that rule tonight. Their friends, brothers and sisters, and some parents were dead. And this was not a mass anyway, it was more like a takeover. It was bringing the streets into the house of God, and finally giving the building some relevance to our lives in Southie. P.J.'s father was on the altar now, not the priest.[7]

Virtually no Catholic clergy appear in the whole of MacDonald's account; one is a Father Murphy who when he learns of the beatings and adulteries of Ma's first husband, tells her, "You're a Catholic, make the best of it."[8] Nuns appear only as schoolteachers who lose

7. Ibid., 10.   8. Ibid., 18.

control of the kids. MacDonald says, "We had a church on the corner that would fill on Sundays, mostly with second graders preparing for First Communion and elderly women."[9] Although his mother has spiritual yearnings and prays "through the Saints and mostly through the Blessed Mother,"[10] she never attends Mass because of her multiple divorces. "The kids"—Ma's collective noun for her large family—attend Mass when young, where they filch the pennies intended for the collection plate.

The community spends a great deal of its time at funerals—at one point Ma realizes that she went to thirty-two in a single year—but it is notable that *All Souls* almost never takes us inside the physical structure of a church. Rather, Jackie O'Brien's funeral parlor is where institutional grieving takes place. There, the usual coffin accessories for "Southie's buried children," MacDonald writes, are "Rosary beads, Irish flags, and shamrock trinkets collected from the annual St Patrick's Day parade."[11] This, indeed, may be the most poignant of all the impoverishments that afflict the underclass residents of Southie: the absence of a meaningful vocabulary with which to understand their inner life and their shared experiences of chaos, loss, and desperation.

These ersatz attempts to invent meaningful traditions and ceremonial gestures bespeak a profound feeling of separation from the larger world and its traditions; among other things, the community misses out on the normative Irish-American narrative of success and acceptance into mainstream society. At one level, the book examines the results of having a conspicuously Catholic ethnic heritage—that of being Irish in Southie—abut the conspicuously secular world of violent, gangster-run streets. Clearly, traditional Catholicism continues to shape the worldviews of the MacDonald family and their neighbors, but in a fashion that is weighted heavily on only one aspect of the conventional understandings of religion as an interplay of "creed, code, and cult."

"Creed" in this schematic refers to "the cognitive aspect of a reli-

9. Ibid., 65.   10. Ibid., 39.
11. Ibid., 186.

gion; it is everything that goes into the 'explanation' of the ultimate meaning of life."[12] It comprises those doctrinal matters of religion that arise from study and debate—the sorts of theological matters to which Catholics assent when they recite the Apostles' Creed.

Such matters are of little concern to the community. In the book's first paragraph MacDonald says of his four buried brothers that "When I accepted the fact that I couldn't feel them at the graves, I figured it must be because they were in heaven, or the spirit world or whatever you want to call it."[13] Admittedly, this sort of befuddlement is something almost anyone might say in such a moment. But the point is that the church's received teachings on life after death are not part of the author's response; there is no theological or eschatological "creed" available to him when he stands before the mysteries of death and the afterlife.

"Code" refers to the expected behaviors that a religion asks of its adherents: moral conduct of all kinds, as well as such explicitly Catholic demands as Mass attendance, reception of the sacraments, and so on. These, too, hold little interest for MacDonald. "Even as a kid," he writes in a moment of reflection, "I always felt torn between the Catholic Church and its rules for who's in and who's out with Jesus, and a deeper relationship with God that might be found anywhere."[14] Daily life in the projects of Southie is anything but moderated by conventional morality. Rather, as MacDonald's mother describes it toward the end of the book, "This place is like fucking Sodom and Gomorrah."[15]

However, the aspect of "cult"—that is, "ritual activities that relate the follower to one aspect or another of the Transcendent, either directly or indirectly"[16]—assumes great importance in the

---

12. Leonard Swidler and Paul Mojzes, *The Study of Religion in an Age of Global Dialogue* (Philadelphia: Temple University Press, 2000), 7. For a discussion of these terms with reference to canon law (where they are also called doctrine, discipline, and ceremonies), see Thomas Richstater, *Liturgical Law Today: New Style, New Spirit* (Chicago: Franciscan Herald Press, 1977), xx–xxiii.

13. MacDonald, *All Souls*, 1.   14. Ibid., 40.

15. Ibid., 219.

16. Swidler and Mojzes, *Study of Religion*, 7.

spiritual landscape of MacDonald's Southie. "Cult" is often discussed by theologians in terms of the sacraments and the theology of the priesthood. Among MacDonald's South Boston neighbors, however, cultic Catholicism thrives in the constellation of traditional practice, material culture, and a semi-magical belief in the potency of such things as holy water. In addition, just as it became a truism to say of the Irish peasantry that Christianity was only a thin veneer over a much older body of folk belief and "elderfaiths," Southie's sense of the supernatural is not always explicitly Catholic or Christian; some verges on the occult.[17]

For instance, as a small boy visiting his brother Davey, who is hospitalized in a psychiatric institution, the narrator realizes that he seems to evoke emotional reactions among the inmates—because, he explains, "I was a seventh son and had special powers only they could read." He goes on to reflect that "I wasn't technically a seventh son since that would probably require one consistent father and God knows we never had one of them."[18] The drug-abusing matriarch of a particularly troubled family in the projects, a Mrs. Meaney, looks strikingly like a witch in her frizzed hair, outsized robes, and bony physique; MacDonald says, "I believed in witches.... Ma and Nellie [an Irish neighbor] had talked about a few people in Ireland who put curses on people."[19] He recounts that his neighbors sincerely feared the Meaney women's powers of "levitating" people and controlling their attack Dobermans through ESP.

Whatever they may believe about the Meaneys, the MacDonald family members themselves believe that they have psychic pow-

17. The ethnographer Lawrence Taylor notes several instances of such persistence of folk belief within Catholic practice in *Occasions of Faith: An Anthropology of Irish Catholics* (Philadelphia: University of Pennsylvania Press, 1995), especially chap. 5, "The Drunken Priest," 145–66. A vast literature concerning Ireland's supposed connections to folk belief and earlier religious traditions, much of it of dubious scholarly value, has emerged among "New Age" writers. However, the subject has lately begun to attract serious scholarship; see Olivia Cosgrove, Laurence Cox, Carmen Kuhling, and Peter Mulholland, eds., *Ireland's New Religious Movements* (Newcastle: Cambridge Scholars Press, 2011).

18. MacDonald, *All Souls*, 38.

19. Ibid., 125.

ers: *All Souls* includes three accounts of prophetic dreams, including one by the narrator himself. On another occasion, the author references a traditional folk belief that it's bad luck for a bird to fly into a house, as a crow did the week before his brother Frank's murder: "The Irish have this thing about birds inside houses; when I was little I couldn't even bring in a picture of one. Once I gave Ma a glass bird to hang on our silver disco Christmas tree and she threw it in the trash, saying it was bad luck."[20]

Not surprisingly, given the nearness of such folk belief, the Catholic traditions most evident in McDonald's Southie—if one excludes the wearing of Notre Dame "Fighting Irish" clothing, which is both ubiquitous and sadly ironic, as few if any of the young people of Southie would ever find their way to ultra-respectable Notre Dame—tend toward the sacramentals, those objects and actions that in some way resemble the sacraments, and that in practice are often ascribed nearly magical powers. Holy water would be a familiar example. In one tragicomic passage in *All Souls* MacDonald and his grandfather attempt to throw holy water from Fatima over the narrator's older sister Kathy, who is comatose and in a protective isolation unit because of her weakened immune system:

Infections were taking over her body, and she had pneumonia. There was no way the nurses were going to let us dump water on her. But this was holy water. . . . The nurses caught Grandpa after he managed to pull the jug from out of his baggy trousers and pour it all over Kathy's head, hands, and feet. Grandpa was shaking and in tears, and he told one nurse to go fuck herself when she came in screaming and trying to pull the old-fashioned jug from his hands. More nurses came running in when they heard the fighting. They started to gang up on him but Grandpa was too strong for them. He kept on reciting the Rosary and telling the nurses in his Irish brogue to shut their fucking mouths.[21]

As a matter of record, a few days later, his sister awakens from her coma and eventually returns home. Later in the book, after losing four children, Ma and her Irish father make a pilgrimage to Fatima,

20. Ibid., 185.   21. Ibid., 170–71.

after which she also adapts an obsession with not only holy water but with stones from the sacred site: "Ma's pocketbook was full of rocks from Fatima. 'Oh thanks ... what's this?' I asked, trying to sound thankful as she handed me a three-pound rock."[22]

Such practices might well appear naïve and even superstitious to outsiders. But in considering the trust that Ma and others place in these objects and practices, it is important to bear in mind the prevailing sense of powerlessness and abandonment in Southie. When Ma shares healing powers of holy water and stones from Fatima, she is at least indirectly asserting some agency in the cure of her own children. As Colleen McDannell demonstrates in *Material Christianity*, using Lourdes water to heal was not only a means of connecting a lay person to a larger sacred power, but also a way of asserting that power does not belong solely to recognized specialists: holy water could impart authority that, in a hospital setting, had been totally ceded to medical experts.[23] Southie, it seems, needs to act as its own guardian angel.

The enduring, although nondoctrinal, Catholic belief in guardian angels dates back to at least the fourth century. The traditional belief is that God designates an angel to each created soul to lead that individual to Heaven by encouraging good thoughts, assisting in prayer, imparting the strength to resist evil, and so on, but the angel is not capable of effecting anything independent of the will of the guarded one.

In popular belief, guardian angels are much more associated with overt acts of intervention and protectiveness; certainly, most American Catholics grew up acquainted with a holy card or print that depicts small children being led safely over turbulent waters, with the steadying hand of an angel on their shoulders. As the *New*

22. Ibid., 201.

23. See Colleen McDannell, *Material Christianity: Religion and Popular Culture in America* (New Haven: Yale University Press, 1995), chap. 5, "Lourdes Water and American Catholicism," 132–62. Crucially, McDannell notes that such practices were not considered aberrant or confrontational by the nineteenth-century medical establishment, which allowed for a range of healing practices. Needless to say, such tolerance was not shown to Ma in Boston City Hospital.

"Someone Watching Your Back"

Catholic Encyclopedia notes, most frequently "guardian angel is taken to mean a single angel assisting an individual man or group of persons, or a single parish, nation, etc."[24]

It is especially important to recognize that guardian angels can be designated for a group, rather than solely for individuals. MacDonald has insisted that the book is not his autobiography, but rather the story of his neighborhood and his family—a point underscored by his subtitle, *A Family Story from Southie*. In *All Souls*, MacDonald's family seizes on the Catholic notion of the guardian angel to respond to at least some of the many losses experienced by the family and the neighborhood.

Ma, of course, is the archetypal angel for her family. Her protectiveness is vividly on display, including in a passage early in the book when she stands guard all night with a sawed-off shotgun. She is also continually engaged in rescue missions to lost souls of men: Michael recalls that "Ma was always trying to save someone from the gutter and that's literally where she met some of her boyfriends. They were usually Irish or Irish-American and often alcoholic and homeless. But before long she'd have them sober and scrubbed up."[25]

More important than Ma's modeling of rescue behavior, though, is the sense of angelic protection that the McDonald family can claim. At several points, Michael Patrick is explicitly given the message that he is being looked after by his older brother, Patrick Michael, who had died at the age of three weeks. For instance, at the age of five, Michael draws a picture of the velvet glow-in-the-dark Last Supper painting in their living room, which his mother extravagantly interprets as a sign of his special spiritual calling:

She said she knew there was something different about me and that it must have something to do with my replacing Patrick Michael. She said she thought he must be very close to me, kind of like a guardian angel. She said that she'd had me to replace him in a way, and that

24. "Angels Guardian (in the Bible)," in *New Catholic Encyclopedia* (New York: McGraw Hill, 1967), 519.

25. MacDonald, *All Souls*, 36.

when she was pregnant with me she'd had a vision of exactly what I'd look like, and that a voice had told her I was a "child of light."[26]

Later, the guardian brother is invoked when Michael is left alone with his mentally ill brother Davey during a terrifying schizophrenic episode. He says, "I prayed to every ancestor I ever heard of, and to my Brother Patrick, and to the Blessed Mother, to intervene and not let Davey kill himself or anything like that."[27]

Significantly, MacDonald recalls that his earliest memory is of seeing his mother crying while sitting on the trunk that her father brought from Ireland—a compelling image of the sadness that has haunted the Irish diaspora. He crawls on her lap and asks her why she is sad, and she replies by telling him that she'd had

a baby who'd died and gone to heaven. She said his name was Patrick Michael, and that it was all going to be okay now because we had someone watching over us, praying for us every day. She told me that I'd taken Patrick Michael's place, and that she'd switched the name around and called me Michael Patrick, because the Irish always said it was bad luck to name a child after another who'd died.[28]

And he notes after that incident, he could "never get mad at her the way most kids did at their parents.... After I saw her cry for Patrick Michael, I only wanted to protect her."[29]

In these exchanges, the MacDonald family appears to adapt the Catholic devotional understandings that Anne Taves has summarized as comprising a "household of faith" to include its own deceased members. As Taves shows, Catholics not only came to model the church and the afterlife in terms of the family, but also to considered the family itself to include spiritual beings. She quotes an 1854 tract by Fr. Frederick Faber that asserts "the angels and saints are all the kindest and most familiar of brothers."[30] For Ma and her children, it is not only the recognized saints who can be called on to

26. Ibid., 38.   27. Ibid., 138.
28. Ibid., 16.   29. Ibid., 17.
30. Ann Taves, *The Household of Faith: Roman Catholic Devotions in Mid-Nineteenth-Century America* (Notre Dame: University of Notre Dame Press, 1986), 48.

facilitate graces and favors, but also the members of her own family who are presumed to be among them.

Certainly, the MacDonald family certainly did not invent the idea that a deceased child looks out for them from heaven. That is a standard trope of Victorian sentimentality and a persistent theme in the literature of consolation.[31] Although the notion of being reunited with family members appears to have gained wide currency with Victorian Protestantism, since the late nineteenth century, American Catholics appear to have grown more and more attracted to the idea that the family would continue in the next life.[32]

Michael Patrick is explicitly told that he has a special connection to an angel in heaven, his deceased brother. And in some longstanding family dynamic—and it should be noted, one that helps to spare him from the unfortunate fates of his siblings—it *does* fall to Michael Patrick to take up the role of the protector. Mindful that he has a named guardian angel looking over him, Michael grows into the role of guardian himself. One of the transformative moments in MacDonald's story comes when, at the age of eleven, he finds himself looking after his new baby brother Seamus. It troubles him when his Southie neighbors use vulgar language in front of a baby:

Seamus was only a few weeks old anyway. It probably didn't matter what he heard; and when they'd come up to the carriage, the same people who'd just called someone a douchebag would start taking baby talk to him and tucking in his blanket. I couldn't help worrying for Seamus, with his brand-new baby smell and brand-new terry cloth baby suits, in the middle of all this anger and confusion and drug-dealing and fighting. I still loved our world at Old Colony, but I wasn't so sure about that now that I had a little brother to wheel around.[33]

The cognitive dissonance that he feels—"I wasn't so sure about that now that I had a little brother to wheel around"—is intensified

31. See Laurence Lerner, *Angels and Absences: Child Deaths in the Nineteenth Century* (Nashville: Vanderbilt University Press, 1997).

32. Bernhard Land and Colleen McDannell, *Heaven: A History* (New Haven: Yale University Press, 1988), 269.

33. MacDonald, *All Souls*, 109.

by the sociological context in which, collectively, the residents of South Boston insist that they live a privileged life. No matter how many social pathologies may afflict their families, or rage right outside their doors, the residents of South Boston insist that they are in fact, uniquely blessed to live in this neighborhood. As MacDonald himself says, they were "comforted by the line that Southie was the one place 'where everyone looks out for each other,'" including, it seems, the dead.[34]

The book opens with MacDonald saying, "I was back in Southie, 'The Best Place in the world,' as Ma used to say before the kids died."[35] This phrase, or near variations, is repeated dozens of times throughout the narrative. At several points, Old Colony is called "A Heaven on earth." On their first day in the Old Colony project, MacDonald's mother "pointed to all the shamrock graffiti and IRA and IRISH POWER spray painted everywhere, and said it looked just like Belfast and that we were in the best place in the world"[36]—a judgment that many residents of Belfast, during those worst years of the Troubles, might have a hard time understanding.

Years later, when he returns to South Boston after a long absence, MacDonald says in an elegiac moment, "That's what we considered ourselves in Southie—Family. There was always this feeling that we were protected, as if the whole neighborhood was watching our back for threats, watching for all the enemies we could never really define. No 'outsiders' could mess with us."[37]

At the start of the busing controversy, the people of Southie are eager to find a political champion: the politician Dapper O'Neill, Whitey's "good brother" Senator Billy Bulger, then Boston committee member Louise Day Hicks are all happy to step in and fill a public role as guardian; at an anti-busing rally, the young Michael hears that Hicks is "the only one sticking up for us."[38] As the great social experiment of forced busing continues, and in the space of a few years the dropout rate among Southie's children approaches

34. Ibid., 135.   35. Ibid., 1.
36. Ibid., 51.   37. Ibid., 2.
38. Ibid., 75.

80 percent, a new guardian angel appears. "Visible or not, we had a hero, a powerful champion, in the midst of all the trouble that enemy forces were heaving on us."[39] Somehow, Whitey Bulger "was the only one left to turn to."[40]

But Whitey, of course, protected no one but himself; and although his power over the neighborhood derived in part from a code of silence in which "snitching" led to certain death, he was in fact being subsidized as an informant throughout the time period described: MacDonald concludes bitterly that "the FBI had sponsored the parade of caskets that passed through the streets of Southie."[41] Far from expelling drugs and other afflictions, Whitey Bulger was vigorously marketing heroin and crack to the young people of the projects. Most of Southie's dead children named in the closing vigil were, as MacDonald never allows us to forget, his victims.

It may be more than mere coincidence that the author of this account is named Michael, like the archangel. In a sense, he has assumed a cultural script that asks him to look for—or to take up the role of—a protecting angel. Indeed, the subconscious linkages to the Archangel Michael are extended by the location chosen for the vigil: the Gates of Heaven Catholic Church, where, rather than swords, the author and his community take up candles. The vigil that opens and closes the book is a ritual of remembrance, a ceremony of healing or at least the start of healing, and in a very real way an exorcism—perhaps not of the evils that continue to plague South Boston and its wounded families, but an exorcism of the silences and lies that sustained these torments.

39. Ibid., 112.
40. Ibid., 111.
41. Ibid., 222. The story of Bulger's informing is described in detail in Dick Lehr and Gerard O'Neill, *Black Mass: The True Story of an Unholy Alliance between the FBI and the Irish Mob* (New York: HarperCollins Perennial, 2000).

9

Picture Windows

Irish-American Memoirs of the Suburbs

Among the American intelligentsia, at least, it's awfully hard to find someone with a good word to say about the suburbs. Our cities may be wholly ringed by suburbs, and have been for half a century now, but to the intellectual classes these newer communities exist as a sort of unadmitted shadow that they are keen to disown.

If meaning only comes clear with hindsight, and if hindsight is the defining quality of memoir, then it is surprising that there are not more memoirs of suburbia. At this point, millions of baby boomers were raised in and dwelled in these places for most of their lives.[1] The suburban environment has been charted in any number of superb novels. Such authors as John Cheever, Joyce Carol Oates, John Updike, and Richard Yates are recognized geniuses in modern American literature, and Sloan Wilson's *The Man*

---

1. In fact, suburbia is graying; see Carl Morello, "If Baby Boomers Stay in Suburbia Analysts Predict Cultural-Shift," *Washington Post,* June 28, 2011, http://www.washingtonpost.com/local/if-baby-boomers-stay-in-suburbia-analysts-predict-cultural-shift/2011/06/27/AGeMLU0H_story.html.

in the Gray Flannel Suit (1955) stands as a masterful rendering of the postwar moment.[2] But the suburbs, thus far, have not given rise to a defining American memoir. Books that put an Irish spin on the story are fewer still. Two that do, however, are David Beers's 1996 *Blue Sky Dream: A Memoir of America's Fall from Grace*,[3] an account of life in the California subdivisions and the rise and fall of the aerospace industry; and Dan Barry's lovely 2004 book, *Pull Me Up: A Memoir*, much of which takes place in Deer Park, Long Island, in the 1960s and 1970s.[4] His story may indeed be the first great memoir of suburbia.

The books by Beers and Barry open a window on what it meant to be Irish in suburbia; they should be read against the widespread assertion by historians of Irish America that suburbs are places where the neighborhoods went to die. One of the harshest such statements of disdain appears in Lawrence McCaffrey's widely cited *The Irish Diaspora in America*, which ends with a chapter entitled "From Some Place to No Place" that takes direct aim at suburbia. Writing in 1976, he concluded that the suburbs are the end of the story. "Irish America," he wrote,

should ask itself whether the price of assimilation and abandoned ethnic identity has been too high. After Vietnam and Watergate, many Irish Americans have come to realize that they probably gave up a great deal for very little; the American mainstream has the stench of an open sewer. Irish America exists in a cultural nowhere. The trip from the old city neighborhoods has been a trip from someplace to no place.[5]

Dermot Quinn's 2004 survey *The Irish in New Jersey* (and New Jersey is the most suburbanized state in the union) begins its final chap-

2. Sloan Wilson, *The Man in the Gray Flannel Suit* (New York: Simon and Schuster, 1955).

3. David Beers, *Blue Sky Dream: A Memoir of America's Fall from Grace* (New York: Harcourt Brace, 1996).

4. Dan Barry, *Pull Me Up: A Memoir* (New York: W. W. Norton, 2004).

5. Lawrence J. McCaffrey, *The Irish Diaspora in America* (Bloomington: Indiana University Press, 1976), 178.

ter, "The End of the Journey," by surveying the Irish in suburbia. "The decade and a half that followed the end of the Second World War was an American Golden Age," he writes. During this age,

> The farms that hemmed America's cities were gobbled up by a vast, unstoppable march, fields turned into suburbs, meadows laid low by golf courses.... A nation at peace had turned its swords not into plowshares but into 5-Irons.... With suburbs stretching to every horizon, Irish Americans surveyed a landscape radically different from that of their parents and grandparents. Tenements gave way to picket fences; backyards became homegrown Edens.[6]

Quinn continues in this vein, concluding that "From city to suburb represented more than a physical journey. Ethnicity itself was transformed. As the Irish became bourgeois, their Irishness changed; the pig in the parlor was now porcelain."[7]

The Irish in New Jersey is more of a documentary history than an interpretive study, but Quinn floats an intriguing idea when he proposes a distinction between Irishness, which is tied to history, and "Irish American-ness," which is tied to heritage, a more elusive concept. His conclusions leave the door open to an understanding of suburbanized ethnicity as, in effect, an adaptive process, arguing that the acceptance of a commodified Stage Irishness pinned on such things as Bing Crosby records is a not a function of cultural annihilation, but rather "a clever calculation."[8] Irishness was protean and could become whatever we wanted it to be, to serve whatever ends it was asked to serve. Still, his overarching narrative is that Irishness essentially ceased to exist once it left the old neighborhood. The bland new world of postwar split-levels is all the more remarkable because it followed so soon after the distinctive milieu of the city.

Trading one for the other often appears, in retrospect, to have

---

6. Dermot Quinn, *The Irish in New Jersey: Four Centuries of American Life* (New Brunswick: Rutgers University Press, 2004), 172.

7. Ibid., 173.

8. Ibid., 176.

Picture Windows

been a bad swap. Tom Hayden's memoir *Irish on the Inside: In Search of the Soul of Irish America* (2001) seeks to explain his radical politics as a welling forth of an unadmitted Irish soul.[9] Hayden is way over- the-top at many points in the book in terms of coercing a historical rationale for his convictions. Yet his book occasionally shimmers with insight. Growing up in suburban Royal Oak, Michigan, Hayden witnessed his parents' and their generation's unquestioning acceptance of the postwar American Dream. In a short subchapter entitled "Suburban Dreams," he characterizes their thinking:

Safety lay in assimilation, blending in, preserving appearances of success and respectability. . . . Respectability was the end of the rainbow for my parents, and it was defined as sending me to the University of Michigan. . . . Assimilation was peaceful ethnocide. . . . Normalcy beckoned after the seeming eternity of trauma [that the Irish had endured]. . . . Respectable assimilation was a mask for other longings. . . . I mirrored my parents' subconscious messages. I simply assumed that these silent family failures were normal, or perhaps the price to pay on the long day's journey to success.[10]

The ironic allusion to O'Neill, in a "long day's journey to success," suggests that Hayden seeks to place himself as yet another Irish-American commentator on the spiritual costs of middle-class comfort.

One of the few books that *is* enthusiastic about the suburbs is Tom Martinson's *American Dreamscape: The Pursuit of Happiness in Postwar Suburbia* (2000).[11] Martinson, an unabashed apologist for suburbia, identifies three broad criticisms of suburbia. The first of these is the aesthetic objection. The unloveliness and widely remarked-upon tediousness of suburban architecture and design is a donée in all commentary on the new housing developments, summed up in Malvina Reynolds's more-than-a-little patronizing 1964 song

9. Tom Hayden, *Irish on the Inside: In Search of the Soul of Irish America* (New York: Verso, 2001).

10. Ibid., 54–55.

11. Tom Martinson, *American Dreamscape: The Pursuit of Happiness in Postwar Suburbia* (New York: Carroll and Graf, 2000).

about the "little boxes made of ticky-tacky." The second is functional. Suburbia, dependent on the automobile, rapacious for land, and defined by freestanding houses, represents a colossally inefficient use of resources, subsumed in the term "sprawl."

It is hard to disagree with the first two sets of objections: the monotonousness and the inefficiency—particularly the latter—seem beyond dispute. But there is a third set of objections that concerns the presumed values and motivations of the individuals who live in suburbia. Much of this discourse assumes that the very raison d'être of suburbia is white flight; that consumerism is the true religion of the suburbs; that suburbia actively discourages a sense of community; and that it is in great and small ways a soul-killing place, if it is a place at all—if we understand "place" in its literary sense of being an environment invested with meaning.

Blue Sky Dream and *Pull Me Up* are two Irish-American works that explicitly take on the challenge of interpreting the suburbs. However homogenous the subdivisions may appear on the outside, they were not utterly uniform, a point that Barry (whose family lived on the unimaginatively named West 23rd Street) stresses early:

Each household on our block possessed its own habits and manner of speech—its own color, in a way. But when blended together, by happenstance or intention, these colors created a new and distinct hue, one not to be found in Commack, or Massapequa, or even on West 22nd Street. It was peculiar to a moment and place in time. . . . You had to be a part of it to see it, this color called West 23rd.[12]

His Deer Park was populated by people who had made a conscious decision to leave the city. "Nearly everyone has migrated from Morningside Heights in Manhattan, Bensonhurst in Brooklyn, Kingsbridge in the Bronx, or some other corner of New York City brick."[13] The word "migrated" is well chosen; the residents of these popped-up communities left behind the familiarity of urban life.

Few of the institutions that gave the largely immigrant city its

12. Barry, *Pull Me Up*, 28.
13. Ibid., 24.

Picture Windows

texture and vitality—institutions where people met one another—survived the trip to suburbia. Family businesses did not; the mom-and-pop grocery turned into a Safeways and 7-Eleven convenience stores. Family occupational traditions, particularly the tradition of multi-generation Irish police and firefighting families from within the neighborhood, did not. Widely used public transportation did not. The corner taverns did not, either; they were succeeded by the class-consciousness and starchy display of the country club. The animated sidewalk and street life that we glimpse in such films as *Going My Way*, with the children playing stickball and hopscotch, could not be reproduced in a landscape without sidewalks.[14]

The cavalcade of city life ended abruptly with the move to suburbia, and, it is worth remembering, it ended by intent. The old institutions were jettisoned. David Beers makes this perceptive comment about how willingly the new suburbanites, his parents' generation, walked away from the old:

Nowadays, when suburbia is often disparaged as a crisis of place cluttered with needless junk and diminished lives, it is worth considering that it was not suburbia's stuff that drew people like my parents to such lands in the first place, but the emptiness. A removed emptiness, made safe and ordered and affordable. An up-to-date emptiness, made precisely for us.

"We never looked at a used house," my father remembers of those days in the early 1960s.[15]

One institution, however, that had the will and the wherewithal to make the move out of the city and into that "up-to-date emptiness" was the Catholic parish. Beers and Barry each devote considerable attention to portraying both the physical structure and the reinvented meanings of the Catholic Church in the new landscape.

Churches have always been, and as today's suburban megachurches show, still are, alert to demographic shifts. In the nineteenth and early twentieth centuries, American Protestant denomi-

14. *Going My Way*, directed by Leo McCarey (1944).
15. Beers, *Blue Sky Dream*, 39.

nations devoted enormous resources into home missions to Catholic immigrants. They understood perfectly well where the action was. In the years of the postwar boom, the Catholic Church was well aware that its American future lay in the new subdivisions. The 1950s were a period of exploding religiosity; more than 60 percent of Eisenhower's Americans belonged to an organized religion, an increase of 300 percent over a century before. One of the most talked-about Catholic books of 1959 was *The Church and the Suburbs*,[16] the first of eventually more than 120 books by Fr. Andrew Greeley, a generally optimistic assessment of the potential for community and religious life in this new American environment. Greeley reported that in the 1950s, new Catholic churches were opening in the United States at a rate of four per week.[17]

Timothy Meagher's *Columbia Guide to Irish American History* notes that "it is difficult to trace American-born Irish residential patterns in the middle of the twentieth century" but observes that after World War II, the movement carried Irish Americans further afield.[18] The Irish-American population was prominent in filling the new non-places of the 1950s. Again, affiliations with Catholic parishes provide a helpful, if porous, measure of ethnicity. The demographics of the postwar suburbs were often strikingly close to those of the "feeder" neighborhoods that had been left behind. Between 1940 and 1965,

the archdiocese of Chicago created seventy-two new churches in the suburbs and twenty-eight on the city's fringes. Those new churches constituted one-quarter of all the archdiocese's parishes and served half of all its Catholics. Few were probably self-consciously Irish and none probably had only Irish members, but many of them, probably most, were made up largely of third- and fourth-generation Irish Americans.[19]

16. Andrew M. Greeley, *The Church and the Suburbs* (New York: Sheed and Ward, 1959).

17. Greeley, *Church and the Suburbs*, 43.

18. Timothy J. Meagher, *The Columbia Guide to Irish American History* (New York: Columbia University Press, 2005), 133.

19. Ibid., 133.

Picture Windows

David Beers came of age in the almost-instant community of Clarendon Manor, California, a suburb that arose in the 1960s to accommodate the influx of employees at Lockheed and other aerospace industries. His memoir is especially valuable for its portrait of that suburban Catholic church in two chapters, "Our Lady of Aerospace" and, later, "Our Lady of Irony." The author's religious upbringing was solely the purview of his Irish Catholic mother, a transplant from the Quad Cities of the Midwest. Describing her religious worldview, he writes,

Rock Island was the sort of Midwest smudge of industry and docks that daily made its people not expect too much, daily required hope and faith. *Where is God? God is everywhere. Even here, especially here.*

Yes, but could the same Catholic God be found if one lived in prefabricated paradise? Would the same Catholic God be there?

This was a popular question in 1960, the year my mother set about answering it, the year we moved to the Valley of Heart's Delight.[20]

Beers notes the skepticism of the 1950s intellectuals about the future of religion and the worriedness of the Catholic leadership, "whose American church had thrived in the cities' ethnic enclaves."[21] Describing the uneasiness of church leaders after turning their backs on the urban milieu, he speculates that

They nervously watched to see if suburban soil would prove as fertile. All of them were very interested in my mother, the Catholic daughter of Rock Island who had gone and married a Protestant Lockheed engineer and now was moving into a brand-new subdivision in Northern California. Could her God withstand the pleasant weather, the booming economy, the faith in progress, the willed rootlessness that drew a generation like her to such places?

My mother, for one, did not see why not.

She did not see why her children could not be raised to be believing Catholics in a space-age cul-de-sac, could not be taught to say without hesitation, *God is everywhere. Even here. Especially here.*[22]

---

20. Beers, *Blue Sky Dream*, 62. 21. Ibid.
22. Ibid., 62–63.

Blue Sky Dream evokes the new aesthetic of Catholicism in the suburbs. He recalls his parish, Queen of Apostles, as "an environment of stackable steel chairs and checkerboard linoleum."[23] It was, he recalls, a place of tape-recorded chimes, an audible symbol of faux tradition.

Interestingly, the Catholicism of the Beers family was not de-ethnicized. But like a church architecture premised on the interchangeability of stackable chairs—and like the aesthetic of suburbia itself—his Irish identity looks ersatz. Beers's experience of conspicuous Irishness has the ring of consumer choice. He recalls,

My mother assumed the task of making us not merely Catholic, but Irish Catholic. Although at least a half-dozen European bloods mixed within us, she decided her children would be Irish like her dead father because, I think, all the up sides to Irishness appealed to her. In inventing an ethnicity for us, she selected only Irish positives, giving us to understand that we were genetically impish and fun-loving, not unlike the leprechauns who lurked in the oleanders she'd just planted along our backyard fence. She made Patrick my middle name, although everyone in the family, by dint of our willed Irishness, was supposedly on special terms with the good St. Pat. Somewhere deep in her closet, my mother kept a stash of green shamrocks and *Kiss Me! I'm Irish!* buttons that came out on St. Patrick's Day; no child left for school without one pinned to his sweater. Like our Catholicness, this was an Irishness free from the scold of the Old World. Ethnicity need not bind one to outmoded tradition. Ethnicity, in this place scrubbed of cultures, was a flexible tool for the enhancement of personal identity.[24]

Here, Beers's mother displays almost precisely the process described by the sociologist Mary C. Waters's respondents in *Ethnic Options: Choosing Identities in America* (1990),[25] a study that fleshes out Herbert Gans's theorizing of "symbolic ethnicity." After extended interviews with Americans who retain a national identity long after the immi-

23. Ibid., 76.
24. Ibid., 69.
25. Mary C. Waters, *Ethnic Options: Choosing Identities in America* (Berkeley: University of California Press, 1990).

Picture Windows

grant generations, Waters finds that "Again and again, the same message comes thorough. You have to have something you can identify with. If it is a 'special' ethnicity, you can be interesting or elite, but nevertheless you must have something."[26] Trappings of Irish identity such as the green beads and St Patrick's Day buttons that his mother so dutifully keeps throughout the year may indeed have "a lack of demonstrable content,"[27] but they speak to deeply felt social needs:

Symbolic ethnicity fulfills this particularly American need to be "from somewhere." Having an ethnic identity is something that makes you both special and simultaneously part of a community. It is something that comes to you involuntarily through heredity, and at the same time it is a personal choice. And it allows you to express your individuality in a way that does not make you stand out from all kinds of other people.[28]

In contrast to Beers, who had only remote family connections to Ireland and was Irish by choice, Dan Barry, who came of age in Deer Park, Long Island, in the 1970s had much more immediate links through his mother, Noreen Minogue Barry of Shanaglish, County Galway. Barry is a Pulitzer-winning *New York Times* reporter. His 2004 memoir *Pull Me Up* warrants reading for many reasons: for its often comic passages; as a cancer recovery narrative; as a love story; as the tale of a career in journalism—but also as a scrupulous portrayal of suburban life.

Of Deer Park itself, he writes—after noting that one of the seminal events recorded in its slim official history is the opening of its first McDonald's in 1971—that "the Deer Park of my youth had the look of a town built in haste, tailored for the harried and lacking in any sense of permanence. There was no downtown center; most of the farms and roadhouse taverns had yielded to the disposable landmarks of our age, the gas stations and auto-part stores, the supermarkets and franchise restaurants."[29] Later, Barry provides a hilarious account of how his neighbors scrambled to distinguish

26. Ibid., 155.
28. Ibid., 150.
27. Ibid., 151.
29. Barry, *Pull Me Up*, 23.

138

their all-but-identical homes from one another with progressively more ludicrous lawn ornaments.

Throughout the book, the author's often haltingly articulated sense of his own Irishness lurks near. Early in the memoir, we learn that Barry's childhood was marked by a powerful hunger for connection to Ireland. His mother returned home only once after emigrating, refused to comment on the contemporary Troubles of the North, and was outwardly, at least, fully Americanized; she was devoted to the music of Johnny Cash. His father, born and raised in New York City, had a hard childhood and, like so many Irish Americans, had seen the catastrophe of the Great Depression firsthand. For all the silence, the Depression and the many losses of their early lives were always in his mother's and father's minds and lay behind what Barry calls "the larger lesson imparted by our parents: life is fragile; take nothing for granted; everything can change in the bat of an eye."[30]

His parents held only an incomplete grasp of their own family history. "Our parents never told us too much about their own heritage," Barry remembers, "partly because they did not know that much ... leaving us with unlinked bits of genealogical gossip and a prop or two."[31] The youthful Barry looked to music for his clues to what it meant to be Irish. He writes of his early fascination with Irish folk music that

we pored over the album covers like cartographers, searching for some Brigadoon-like portal through which to join the strapping men portrayed on the covers, men with sweaters the color of sea foam and smiles of Celtic confidence: the Clancy Brothers—Liam Pat and Tom—and Tommy Makem. I placed the needle down gently to find the groove. And then we sang, raising our young voices to join tenors and baritones in the ballad of an inebriate, a song whose infinite sadness was masked in a rousing defiance.

30. Ibid., 45.
31. Ibid., 19.

Picture Windows

The song, in fact, was the innocuous favorite "The Jug of Punch," which is an old music hall number and thus not really a traditional tune at all. Barry wonders aloud, "But why did we sing them?" and he concludes by asking, not exactly rhetorically, "was it for us, the children of Eugene and Noreen Barry—Brian, Brenda, Elizabeth, and me, the eldest? To help us in piecing together how we came to be, and how we came to be here on Long Island, in a place called Deer Park?"[32]

The place evoked in *Pull Me Up* is also one in which the suburbanizing church reinvents itself to a new physical and social geography. In this case, the buildings of Sts. Cyril and Methodius do not emerge fully formed, but come out of a history. "For many years," he recalls, "a small clapboard chapel had provided more than enough space for the Catholics in our area. Then came the New York City throngs of the 1950s, the Barrys and Bernardis and Boyles, buying houses, having babies, cramming into the chapel's pews. . . . The parish had no choice but to build."[33]

Barry describes the rapid construction of the new church in the summer of 1963 and its blessing by the bishop of the diocese of Rockville Centre. On the day of the bishop's visit, he writes, "It was a special morning, after all, a morning in which a young Catholic community had formally anchored itself to the Long Island soil." Barry describes the powerful sense of arrival that attended the new suburban life:

this they knew; their new and holy place, their church, would loom over Deer Park Avenue for generations to come, the parish rolls forever inscribed with the names of the beauticians and car mechanics who financed its construction back in 1963, the new Sts. Cyril and Methodius generated so much community pride that when a formal dance was planned to celebrate the church's blessing and dedication, nearly two hundred people volunteered to be on the dance committee.[34]

32. Ibid.   33. Ibid., 56–57.
34. Ibid., 58.

The small businesses that built the church did not survive into the new millennium. Within a few months of the church's dedication, the Roman Catholic world received a stunning emotional blow with the murder of John F. Kennedy. But for a time in the mid-1960s, he notes, "the Sts. Cyril and Methodius complex, a kind of office park of religious design, had become an accepted part of the Deer Park infrastructure—and a second home for children like me."[35] Perhaps the youthful Fr. Greeley's enthusiasm for the suburbs was not so naïve, after all.

Memoirists like Beers and Barry complicate the conventional wisdom that "the little boxes made of ticky-tacky" are bereft of meaning. These authors are well aware of the conformity and superficiality of suburbs; but their books demonstrate that a soulless place does not inevitably create a soulless populace. Beers and Barry are each conscious that suburbia represented a sort of dream for his parents' generation, and each book is ultimately shot through with yearning and with disappointment. But Clarendon Manor and Deer Park were nonetheless knowable places, both formative and unique to the persons who lived there. And the narrators understand their lives in suburbia as tied to specific historical moments.

For the Beers family in the California subdivisions, their pick-and-choose, ornamental Irishness is both an attempt to connect with their own past (however silly or superficially it may express itself on St. Patrick's Day) and an assertion of a small difference that sets them apart from others in a positive way. For the Barrys of Long Island, their link to Ireland is closer, through their mother's immigration and their father's choice to leave the city behind.

Barry's *Pull Me Up* in particular gives us a valuable window on the processes by which place—including the place of a postwar suburb—creates meaning. The book opens with his mother, far advanced with terminal cancer, in front of an emblematic suburban home accoutrement, the picture window "deep in the living room

35. Ibid., 57.

couch that had been her place all those years."[36] It closes with Barry himself, in his early forties, on the pier in Kinvara, County Galway, having recovered from tracheal cancer, feeling utterly at home and grateful for "the sting of a saltwater blessing upon my face."[37] For Barry, as for numerous recent Irish-American memoirists, Ireland functions as a sort of landscape of both origins and of healing.

Would he feel this so strongly if he had not been raised in the deracinating subdivisions of suburbia? We can only speculate.

What does seem certain is that in our time Ireland has powerfully come to offer such an alternative landscape on which to project our wished-for other lives—the sort of place that Gaston Bachelard, in *The Poetics of Space,* calls "'Eulogized space'—a landscape of memory whose idealization contrasts with the banality of contemporary, workaday landscapes."[38] In the decades that followed World War II, that idealization of Ireland by Americans accelerated—partly because there was some basis in reality, and partly because of the systematic positioning of the country by Irish tourism planners. We might ask, though, whether Americans were particularly ready to entertain Ireland as such an alternative to our daily realities because it was being proposed in the very years that the seeming placelessness of suburbia was consuming the American landscape.

36. Ibid., 9.
37. Ibid., 321.
38. Gaston Bachelard, quoted in Robert Beuka, *SuburbiaNation: Reading Suburban Landscapes in Twentieth-Century American Fiction and Film* (New York: Palgrave MacMillan, 2004), 28.

10

Secular Pilgrimages

Recent Irish-American Memoir and Journeys of Healing

In the summer of 1973, the radio airwaves of America were awash with the clear tenor voice of the young folksinger John Denver singing "Rocky Mountain High," a song that exulted about a young man who "was born in the summer of his twenty-seventh year / Coming home to a place he'd never been before."

Perhaps that phrase, "coming home to a place he'd never been," was unfamiliar to America at large, but for Irish Americans, it was nothing new. They had been uttering it for years.

The frequency with which they said it increased exponentially after regularly scheduled jet service from New York to Shannon began in 1958. The ease of transatlantic travel marked a decisive turning point in the systematic development of Irish tourism, giving rise to a boom that has only modestly stopped booming since.[1] Stories in American periodicals that had been placed with help from

---

1. For an excellent account of the development of the Irish travel industry, see Eric Zuelow, *Making Ireland Irish: Tourism and National Identity since the Irish Civil War* (Syracuse: Syracuse University Press, 2009).

Secular Pilgrimages

Bord Fáilte, the Irish tourist board, often spoke of Ireland as possessing a "something in the air" that spoke to the heart and souls of the travelers. And in an extraordinary number of these accounts—and a great many accounts from before the systematic marketing of tourism—we hear exactly the language of John Denver's smug little song, that of coming home-where-we-have-never-been; indeed, if one reads at any length in this literature, the report of an instant "oceanic" connection to Ireland appears almost unavoidable.

In 1949, for instance, the *New Yorker* writer John McNulty, well known for his Runyonesque stories of the Irish bars of Manhattan, wrote a longish account of a two-month stay in Ireland—an account full of booze and Stage Irishry—that he titled, "Back Where I Had Never Been."[2] In the 1950s, for instance, the future novelist Thomas Flanagan, author of the *Year of the French*, made his first trip to Ireland, where he had a life-changing epiphany.[3] He writes, "I felt a clear, breathless and unified moment of personal identity" in which he had a "powerful sense, never afterward to leave me, that some deep and essential part of my being had found its way to its home."[4]

In a much more prominent "roots trip" in June of 1962, no less a figure than President John F. Kennedy said, during his visit to New Ross, County Wexford, that "It is strange that so many years could pass and so many generations pass and still some of us who came on this trip could come home—here to Ireland—and feel ourselves at home and not feel ourselves in a strange country."[5] Admittedly, these examples are from fifty years ago and more. Many of the

2. John McNulty, "Back Where I Had Never Been," *New Yorker*, September 10, 1949.

3. Thomas Flanagan, *The Year of the French* (New York: Holt, Rinehart, Winston, 1979).

4. Flanagan, "One American Irish Identity," in *There You Are: Writings on Irish and American Literature and History*, ed. Christopher Cahill (New York: New York Review of Books, 2004), 439.

5. John F. Kennedy, "Remarks at Eyre Square, Galway, June 29, 1963," *Public Papers of the Presidents of the United States: John F. Kennedy, 1963* (Washington, D.C.: Government Printing Office), 540.

writers are the children or grandchildren of immigrants at a time when the transatlantic networks were in some ways more fresh and a child might grow up hearing about Ireland on a daily basis. What is intriguing, though, is that the formulation of Ireland as a "homecoming" to somewhere you had never been shows no sign of abating.

The internet abounds with blogs and travel sites in which tourists echo this idea. There are any number of sites compiled by college students after a study-abroad experience. In one, entitled, "Eleven Tales to Inspire Your First Trip to Ireland," we find such comments as these: "any tiredness disappeared as soon as the wheels touched down and I was in Ireland. Immediately I felt at home." Another wrote, "I felt in love with Ireland many years ago. . . . I can probably say, I fell in love before I was born . . . today I arrive in Ireland and there is something making me feel like home."[6]

In 2013, Áine Greaney, an Irish-born writer now living in Massachusetts, posted a thought-provoking column on the *Irish Abroad* site entitled, "Is Ireland Really Home?" Readers responded with a wide range of comments, among them an Eileen MacNamara, who wrote, "Ireland is my heart's home, although I live in the U.S." This, in turn, evoked a reply from a Mr. Mulhern that "My 'home' is in Ireland. Although never visited until late in life, this became very apparent as we approached landing in Dublin. An overwhelming feeling of warmth and familiarity came over me as I watched the coast approach." A Katy Abraham also wrote in to speak for "those of us who were born here in the states but feel like Ireland is home? . . . each time I step off the plane my heart says Home." And a William Sherlock who had been to a family reunion under the auspices of "The Gathering"—a 2013 tourism initiative intended to "call back" the diaspora—reported that "There were over 250 extended family members present from all corners of the globe and spread over 5 generations with 3 more in the local graveyard. A good number had

---

6. "Eleven Tales to Inspire Your First Trip to Ireland," http://www.infiniteire land.com/tales-to-inspire-your-first-trip-to-ireland/.

never been to Ireland before but all felt they had come home."[7] One could list such comments ad infinitum.

How can a place that has never been seen elicit such strong recognitions?

One possible explanation that has a lot of appeal to our skeptical age is that this perception is bogus. This position holds that the emotion is at bottom a constructed channeling of tourists' expectations: roots tourists go to Ireland looking for, and therefore finding, ways to fulfill the implanted suggestion. The marketing of Irish tourism, like the marketing of tourism to any country, is predicated on the premise that destinations are not fungible: that one travels to Ireland precisely because certain experiences available there are not available elsewhere. For travelers from the diaspora, there is an overtly stated claim that one of those experiences will be a form of "return," an idea implicit in the "Gathering" campaign. As Stephanie Rains notes in *The Irish-American in Popular Culture, 1945–2000*,

it is this concept, which recurs again and again within filmic and touristic depictions of Ireland for the 1950s onward, of going "back" for the first time, of the possibility of a "return" to a place which has not yet been visited, which illuminates the construction of Ireland by and for its diaspora through film imagery, and which is so vividly displayed in the development of the Irish tourist industry.[8]

Yet another approach would be to explain this phenomenon in postcolonial terms, in terms of exile, and of the colonizer having so extensively displaced or drowned out the culture of the colonized to the point where it becomes more like home than home itself. Ho Chi Minh, for instance, wrote of how troubled he was to visit Paris as a young man, where he worked as a waiter, and find that it was more familiar to him than his own Vietnam: Ho identifies this realization as a turning point in the emergence of his nationalism. This seems easy enough to accept—though one might wonder the

7. Áine Greaney, *"Is Ireland Really 'Home?' Used to Be? Wanna be? Never Be?"* http://www.irishabroad.com/Blogs/Posts.aspx?date=2013–09&bid=31398.

8. Stephanie Rains, *The Irish-American in Popular Culture, 1945–2000* (Dublin: Irish Academic Press, 2007), 101–2.

extent to which a colonial dynamic can be applied to American college students.

Other explanations suggest themselves. Trauma theory might have something to say about this or about Freud's explanation of the repetition compulsion. And there are other notions that would be very persuasive, if accepted, with which this article will not engage: reincarnation, for instance, which would allow for past life recognition. Or the notion of cell memory. Or ghosts.

Yet, before we look to psychoanalysis, postcolonial analysis, or trauma theory, there are a couple of old ideas that might helpfully be brought into the conversation. One is the archetypal notion of pilgrimage to a much greater extent than is generally recognized, travel to Ireland is framed in the language of a quest for restoration, and thus, of pilgrimage.

There is another quite familiar idea that might also speak to this phenomenon: the psychology of attraction, and specifically, that of love at first sight. Much of the research literature on the phenomenon concerns pheromones and sexual attraction—but not all of it. Particularly intriguing is the frequently presented idea that love at first sight is a product of one person (the one falling) investing the other with the potential for effecting some sort of a spiritual transformation. Although it is a perspective rarely heard from in Irish Studies, I would suggest that we might learn something from an approach to couples counseling known as Imago Therapy, developed by Harville Hendrix. Though by no means concerned solely with love at first sight, the core idea of Harville's approach is that attraction is explained by the power of preconscious, or unconscious, perceptions that we ascribe to the person with whom we fall in love, however accurately or inaccurately.

Importantly, this often inchoate soup of ideas about the other is not, as Hendrix writes, confined to linear time; in love "Today, Tomorrow, and Yesterday do not exist; everything that was, still is."[9] Holding these ideas in place—the notion of pilgrimage, the no-

---

9. Harville Hendrix, *Getting the Love You Want: A Guide for Couples* (New York: Macmillan, 2001), 13.

tion of time being nonlinear and somehow running differently in Ireland than it does elsewhere, and the notion of our pursuit of an unconscious fit—will be very helpful as we look at the literature of return.

Such ideas are very much present in a 2006 interview with Katie Holmquist, a young novelist (not of Irish descent) who grew up in Baltimore and now lives in Dublin, which appeared in the *Irish Times*. She was asked about how she happened to be drawn to Ireland, and replied:

Here's a strange story: Never in my childhood did I have a connection to Ireland. Yet, on my first flight to Europe, heading for Paris, I had one of those moments whose significance becomes clear only in later life. We flew over the Shannon, and the pilot pointed out the Cliffs of Moher. I looked down from the tiny window and was overcome by emotion. It was as if everything I had ever lost was somewhere down on that island, and as if I was a grieving angel, looking down on a past life, beginning, middle, and end.[10]

Psychoanalysts have noted the phenomenon of an analysand investing his or her therapist with an almost mystical level of insight; the term is "the one who is presumed to know."[11] Holmquist appears to suggest that she understands Ireland to be somehow the repository of a special knowledge that she herself has not had—the one, or more accurately, the place, that is "presumed to know." It is not that necessary for there to be an actual bestowal of wisdom; it is only necessary that the traveler approach the land as if this bestowal were possible, or somehow more likely. The mere fact that the traveler is, in effect, "buying into" the dream allows the reality of coming home where one has never been to come to pass.

In fairness, it should be noted that a dark image of Ireland is easy to find in the extensive literature of the "Returned Yank"; those stories of an Irish-born individual who comes back to the

10. Kate Holmquist, "Falling in Love with Ireland," *Irish Times* (magazine section), September 2, 2006.
11. Jane Gallop, *Reading Lacan* (Cornell: Cornell University Press, 1985), 44.

land of his or her nativity after a long time away has long appeared in Irish fiction, drama, and film. Despite the stereotype of the romanticized American with green-tinted glasses, the literary record suggests that the experience of return is often unsettling and disillusioning. In George Moore's short story "Home Sickness" (1903),[12] the rediscovered claustrophobia of Ireland forces the protagonist to flee both Ireland and his fiancée, only to be haunted by memories of both for the rest of his days. For many, John Ford's classic 1952 film *The Quiet Man*, based on a 1933 short story by the Irish writer Maurice Walshe, is synonymous with a treacly vision of Ireland;[13] yet, the reality is that the central character, Sean Thornton (John Wayne) grows quickly disenchanted with the romance of his reclaimed home and grows more brutal, less principled the longer he stays in Ireland—a process one recent critic refers as a "searing depiction" of Ireland's capacity to prey on the sentimental.[14] Among autobiographers, one of the most celebrated, and poignant, such accounts appears in *'Tis* (1999),[15] Frank McCourt's follow-up to the blockbuster *Angela's Ashes* (1996), in which McCourt comes back to Limerick in his GI's uniform expecting to treated as a glamorous exotic, only to find that the Irish ignore him or worse.

In recent years, there has been a highly specific recent refinement in the literature of return: a surprising number of Irish-American autobiographies and memoirs relate more gratifying outcomes and moments of insight, explicitly arising from a trip to Ireland. The works discussed are not necessarily memoirs in which Ireland or Irishness features prominently, and the narrator is not an immigrant, but rather an immigrant's descendant—often one several generations removed from Ireland. Each account involves a narrator who is an adult traveling to Ireland with an aging parent.

12. George Moore, "Home Sickness," in *The Untilled Field* (Gerrards Cross: Colin Smythe, 2000), 21–31.

13. *The Quiet Man*, directed by John Ford (1952).

14. Michael Patrick Gillespie, *The Myth of an Irish Cinema: Approaching Irish-Themed Films* (Syracuse: Syracuse University Press, 2008), 116.

15. Frank McCourt, *'Tis: A Memoir* (New York: Scribner's, 1999).

Secular Pilgrimages

And—although the context in which these accounts arise is, super-ficially, that of present-day tourism in which the trip is one of short duration—the narrative trajectory replicates some aspects of classic accounts of pilgrimage in which personal, even spiritual, discoveries persist and transform the individual's understanding of his or her own life long after the trip is concluded.

Before turning to the first-person accounts, it is worth noting that from Thanksgiving week of 1999 until just after St. Patrick's Day, 2001, millions of American television viewers encountered a brief but memorable rendering of this story in the form of a sixty-second MasterCard advertisement in the company's famous "Price-less "series."

The commercial presents an attractive thirty-something wom-an accompanying her mother to Ireland. Visually, scenes of the mother and daughter's trip are interspersed with black-and-white flashbacks of a child playing in an Irish farmyard, presumably the mother in the scenes of her youth (although an alternative reading would be that the child is the daughter who left Ireland at an early age). The familiar voiceover runs as follows: *Plane tickets to Ireland: $1200. Train fare to the town where your mother was born: $63. Drinks at the pub where she met your father: $8. Finally finding out where your mother is coming from: Priceless.*

Shot on locations near Dublin by the distinguished director Jim Sheridan—whose films include *My Left Foot* (1999) and *In Amer-ica* (2003)—the commercial succeeds brilliantly in doing what the MasterCard campaign has always done, which is to link the rela-tively modest, quantifiable expenses that will show up on a credit card statement to larger and incalculably more valuable human connections. Since 1997, the commercial syllogism of the "Price-less" campaign has entered the lingua franca of our times, and not surprisingly, many brief tales told in these commercials involve travel to emotionally resonant places (other spots in the series in-volve a father-and-son ballpark tour, a trip to India, and an ironic advertisement concerning a father-son trip to "roots tour" Scandi-navia). None of the "Priceless" advertisements, or any of the works discussed here, involves solitary travel, and indeed, tourism statistics indicate that more than three-quarters of all tourists to Ireland arrive with at least one other traveling companion. Family members account for some 60 percent of these traveling companions.[16] In other words, the traveler's experience of Ireland is in most cases a shared experience.

The accounts may share a common geographical destination, but in no case is the payoff of the story a greater knowledge of Ireland itself. Instead, the emotional revelations and personal epiphanies with which the authors return from their trips always take the shape of having gained a new and deeper understanding about their own family of origin. This focus on the personal discovery by itself represents a significant departure from the prevailing motif of Irish autobiography, which, as Liam Harte has noted, has been characterized by the national metonymy: "the master trope of the Irish autobiographical tradition: the symbolic refraction of the life of the individual through the lens of nation and society."[17] In the works considered here, however, the movement runs in the opposite direction: these authors look to the national experience only to elucidate their particular family and what they, themselves have experienced as members of that unique constellation of relationships. Because they are at least one generation removed from Ireland, their experience of the country is necessarily filtered through a mother, father, or relative even more distant in time. It is the mystery of the self or the self within a family, and not the experience of a group within its historical contexts, that is to be explained by the memoir.

Such a narrative of family illumination was in the mind of the woman who wrote the MasterCard advertisement. When asked about the origins of the spot, Joyce King Thomas, the president and

16. See Bernd Biege, "Who Visits Ireland? Tourism Statistics—Who Does What Where in Ireland," http://goireland.about.com/od/preparingyourtrip/qt/statistics.htm.

17. Liam Harte, "Introduction: Autobiography and the Irish Cultural Moment," in *Modern Irish Autobiography: Self, Nation and Society*, ed. Liam Harte (Houndsmills and New York: Palgrave MacMillan, 2007), 3.

chief creative officer of the McCann-Erickson agency in New York and the creator of the entire "priceless" campaign, reported that

> The story was inspired by a personal story. . . . My mother was born in Casablanca and met my father, an American in the Air Force, there. They married and he brought her back to his home town, Marshfield, Missouri. She never went back to Casablanca since most of her family, Sephardic Jews, left in the '60s. So, I think this portion of her life has always been a mystery to me. It is easier to picture your parent's childhood when you visit their parents, see their home town, see their interaction with the places of their past. This never happened for my mother and I.
>
> I moved the story to Ireland because it seemed it would be relevant to a larger percentage of the population. Ireland just sounded romantic.[18]

The decision to locate this commercial in Ireland thus partakes in both the pragmatic level of demography and in the romantic, the idea that Ireland is somehow more spiritually aware than other countries.

Since at least the time of the Yeatsian Celtic Twilight, Ireland has often been popularly considered a place of distinctly spiritual associations. This tradition persists in an extreme form in present-day New Age tours of Ireland that unabashedly promise spiritually enlightening trips to "Thin Places." None of the authors considered here, however, state or even suggest that they are consciously seeking any sort of revelation or personal growth as they set out to travel to Ireland. Nonetheless, the shaping pressure of nostalgia, the construction of Ireland as a definingly "green," even prelapsarian place, and for some authors perhaps also the consciousness of exile that attends any diasporic experience all work to freight any trip to Ireland with some heavy cultural and conceptual baggage.

Holmquist's recollection that in looking down on Ireland, "It was as if everything I had ever lost was somewhere down on that island, and as if I was a grieving angel, looking down on a past

18. Joyce King Thomas, e-mail correspondence with author, May 23, 2007.

life, beginning, middle, and end," introduces two themes that run throughout the memoirs of parent-child travel: grief and the sense that one's life takes on a new wholeness. Viewing the MasterCard commercial, it is easy to fill in the gaps with assumptions about what has gone into the story. We know the daughter is motivated by something other than mere holidaying. Throughout, the younger woman looks on with evident astonishment, affection, empathy, appreciation. We witness a scene in which the daughter gains a long-denied knowledge. What we are looking at, in other words, is a reckoning with the enforced silences of Irish life; the playing child suggests that the real purpose of this trip is to confront or reclaim the past, a past that until this trip was unadmitted. The daughter did not understand, and now she does.

But the MasterCard story differs in a crucial respect from the memoir accounts. Implicit in the commercial is the suggestion that what has prevented the realization of the emotional bonds of love and intimacy between mother and daughter has been financial exigency; they either could not afford, or did not think they could afford, the trip. Now, through the magic of the credit card, that impediment is presented as having been miraculously removed.

Significantly, whereas the advertisement presents the trauma of the parent-child relation as having been magically resolved, the memoirs foreground the working-through of that trauma. The authors come to view the trips described as an opportunity to see their own family clearly for the first time. In certain senses, these memoirs resemble the dynamic of Freud's repetition compulsion—the return, driven by one's unconscious, to situations and material that have never been fully understood.

In "Finding Home: Aughkiltubred, 1969," James Murphy declares, "This is the story of his journey home. I went with him and met myself."[19] Christine Cusick introduces "Tourmakeady Snow" by noting the gaps in the family history; she says of her grandfather:

19. James Murphy, "Finding Home: Aughkiltubred, 1969," in *Extended Family: Essays on Being Irish American from "New Hibernia Review,"* ed. James Silas Rogers (Chester Springs, Pa.: Dufour Editions, 2013), 41.

Secular Pilgrimages

He passed away seven years before I was born; and yet even as a child, intrigued by the mysterious absence that I now understand as death, this man I would never know fascinated me.

It wasn't until I was an adult that I would learn that despite living with him for close to two decades, my father actually didn't know much more about his father than I did.[20]

Like the young woman in the MasterCard advertisement, Cusick has lived with an enigma that she may not even have known was puzzling her until the transformative trip. And as her essay closes, Cusick eloquently reflects on the links between the scholar's understanding of Ireland that her academic career has brought and the more organic emotional, even spiritual growth that the trip with her father brought: "I have an acute awareness that the family story that I have to tell is in no way spectacular or extraordinary. We all have stories of loss that define us, and that are hopefully colored by healing. But through this telling I have discovered that before I can fully confront the lessons of literature, I must first be able to listen to the lessons of my own place."[21]

As Cusick makes clear, the sort of learning spoken of in these accounts is personal and interior. Such learning comes in occasions when rationality does not suffice, when other ways of knowing take over. In other words, the trip led her not merely to knowledge, but to wisdom.

As such, the journeys undertaken in the memoirs discussed here become, in some ways, secular iterations of religious pilgrimage. These parent-child "return" voyages represent a secularized, internalized version of the pilgrimage, where the healing occurs at a psychological level and in a therapeutic form. In the Western tradition, pilgrimages were usually undertaken as penances, intended to set things right; a powerful recent expression of this is Seamus Heaney's *Station Island* (1984), a Dantean account of an Irish Catholic pilgrimage in which the poet encounters a range of "shades" from

20. Christine Cusick, "Tourmakeady Snow," in Rogers, *Extended Family*, 49.
21. Cusick, "Tourmakeady Snow," 60.

the past.[22] Further, although pilgrimage almost by definition asserts that certain places are special, different from the ordinary run of the world, there has always been an understanding that in pilgrimage the journey itself, and not just its destination, is a part of the experience. However compromised these spiritual goals may have been along the road—as Chaucer's bickering and bawdy characters show—such trips were intended to be reflective. And though not every pilgrimage is to Lourdes, undertaken to be healed, in these accounts Ireland is in almost every case a post-traumatic destination.

The psychologist Elizabeth Weiss Ozorak notes that contemporary pilgrimages with a religious destination often follow a personal upheaval: "there are many who undertake the journey in an open-ended spirit of exploration, often in response to some personal turning point, such as retirement, divorce, ordination, serious illness, or bereavement."[23] The pattern is unmistakable. Murphy travels with his father back to his hometown forty-five years after the dad emigrated, but "a year after the death of my mother, many years after the death of his own mother and father."[24] Cusick goes to Ireland with her father a little more than a year after his wife, her mother, has died. In works discussed later in this chapter, Michael Patrick MacDonald brings his mother to Ireland after the MacDonalds have endured the deaths of three siblings, had another sister suffer lasting brain damage, and seen a younger brother imprisoned falsely. Patricia Hampl's trip to Ireland with her mother happens soon after the mother recovers from a mastectomy. Peter Quinn's mother planned her trip to Ireland a year after she was widowed. In *Chasing the Hawk*, the Sheehan family holds a reunion in Donegal at the request of their dying father, who has returned to his family after a painful separation:

22. Seamus Heaney, *Station Island* (London: Faber and Faber, 1984).

23. Elizabeth Weiss Ozorak, "The View from the Edge: Pilgrimage and Transformation," in *On the Road to Being There: Studies in Pilgrimage and Tourism in Late Modernity* (Leiden: Koninklijke Brill NV, 2006), 62.

24. Murphy, "Finding Home," 41.

Secular Pilgrimages

In his once-again undisputed role as head of the household he had decreed that there should be large gatherings of all the Sheehans. Further, they should not be in Ocean Grove but in places we hadn't been before, where there would be explorations and a sense of specialness. The first of these would be in Ireland, once a legacy to be fled, now a place to be reclaimed for his own.[25]

In Daniel Tobin's poem "My Mother at the House of Her Father's Father," no sadness or tragedy are fresh in the family's mind when he goes back to Ireland with his mother and father—but he takes the trip fully aware that, because of their aging, "it was now or never."[26]

> This was my idea, to arrange her return
> To where she'd never been, or had been only
> In the myth she made of her life, daughter
> Of a father she storied into legend,
> The pursuing ghost of her fraught affections[27]

Tobin proves right about the impending loss; both would die within a few years of the trip; he says of his mother, "Inside a year she'll be nearly dead, heart-failed, self starved"[28]—but wrong about the hoped-for epiphany, as he speaks of

> historical knowledge my mother
> would have little of. "That's interesting,"
> she'd say, then turn back to what she knew—
> a cultivated picture of her past
> rehearsed in stories on holidays,
> told as lessons, truth be told, to keep us
> from becoming what she could not control,
> my refusal a scar among the other scars
> unspoken.[29]

25. Andrew Sheehan, *Chasing the Hawk: Looking for My Father, Finding Myself* (New York: Delacorte Press, 2002), 253–54.

26. Daniel Tobin, telephone conversation with author, June 5, 2007.

27. Tobin, "My Mother at the House of Her Father's Father," *The Narrows* (New York: Four Way, 2005), 26.

28. Ibid., 28.

29. Ibid., 27.

Tobin's work conveys a sense that loss has been inescapable; he seems to want to make a universal statement about the psychic costs of immigration, finding in the history of migration a metaphor for the reality that we are all involuntary emigrants from the land of childhood into the hurt world of adulthood. In general, though, the communities spoken about in these accounts are the smallest possible: the dyad of parent and child, told from the perspective of the child alone.

Michael Patrick MacDonald's *Easter Rising* is not precisely a sequel to *All Souls*, his 1999 memoir of the South Boston busing controversy and its aftershocks. The second book is far more autobiographical and reflective.[30] Whereas the protagonist of the first book was in a sense the entire MacDonald family and the community of Southie itself, the second book is interior, a chronicle of how he came to be the person he is. MacDonald—who earned a degree in Irish Studies from the University of Massachusetts—makes a strong connection between Irish history and his own inner life. He told *Irish America* magazine:

Knowing where we come from is as important as . . . knowing our genetic history. I was raised by someone and she was raised by someone, and somewhere in there the famine happened and the Easter Rising and the Black and Tans. So history is really wrapped up in how we're raised. People who don't know where the chip on their shoulder comes from don't know why they hit out at black kids on buses.[31]

In traveling to Ireland, then, MacDonald approaches Ireland as if it holds an explanatory power.

Easter Rising closes with MacDonald recounting a trip in which he takes his mother to Ireland with him. The mother, whose father was an immigrant longshoreman, dominates the first book as the

30. MacDonald, *Easter Rising: An Irish American Coming Up from Under* (Boston: Houghton Mifflin, 2006).

31. Lauren Byrne, "A Southie Homecoming: Michael Patrick MacDonald Talks to Lauren Byrne about Growing Up in South Boston," *Irish America Magazine*, February–March 2007.

family's anchor. She does, however, also show a genius for embarrassing her son on both sides of the water. Much of MacDonald's memoir is precisely about how we love our families despite—or even because of—their goofiness and their inadequacies; a barroom musician, "Ma" belts out Irish rebel songs in a London train station, and she hauls her accordion with her across Ireland and breaks into "Danny Boy" at the drop of a hat. Most poignant, in Ireland MacDonald comes to realize the extent to which his mother had previously concealed her fragility—how, unknown to him, she had come close to suicide during the years of nightmare when his family was being ripped apart by drugs and violence in South Boston.

In an affecting scene as the book closes, Michael and Ma encounter a Mr. and Mrs. Wren outside a church. Michael is astonished to find that days before, while visiting a friend's gravesite, his mother had noticed that a young man named Jerry Wren was recently buried nearby. Now, upon meeting his parents, total strangers to her, Ma forms an instant and extraordinary bond springing from the shared experience of having lost a child. Michael says,

I still couldn't get over the fact that while I was focused on how I should and shouldn't behave at Danny's grave, Ma had been observing the details of Jerry Wren's stone. I no longer felt I'd missed out on something by not seeing the bullet-riddled columns of the General Post office. Ma made more sense to me now, and so did all the rebellion, the fights, the transformation of pain into stories that could be sung, in Ireland's history.[32]

The national experience is present here, but it is understood as secondary and subordinate to the personal: MacDonald quite simply states that iconic sites of the national experience are less important than human connections that only those who have suffered the loss of a child can know. The person-to-person bridge that Ma forms with the Wrens through grief becomes, in turn, an opportunity for MacDonald himself to understand his mother's sometimes baffling behavior.

32. MacDonald, *Easter Rising*, 244.

Secular Pilgrimages

Patricia Hampl's *The Florist's Daughter* is solidly anchored in the author's Midwestern home town of St. Paul, Minnesota.[33] Hampl had launched her considerable literary reputation largely on the basis of her 1999 memoir of Prague, *A Romantic Education*.[34] Despite the reference to her Czech-American father in the title of her second book, *The Florist's Daughter* chiefly concerns Hampl's relationship with her Irish-American mother, an ardent Hibernophile. One of the key episodes in the book involves a trip to Ireland that Hampl reluctantly takes at her mother's insistence.

To Hampl's surprise, the trip proves delightful; her mother, she says, "was the best travel companion of my life."[35] In an Irish bed-and-breakfast, Hampl—by that point in her life already a much-honored literary figure—falls into a conversation with her mother about what she had wanted to be when younger. She learns instead that she has spent her own life pursuing her mother's unfulfilled dream:

> But in the little room in the Kilkenny B and B, when I asked her what she wanted to be as a girl, she looked at me from her twin bed, tucked up in her cotton jammies, and said in disbelief, "You don't know?"
>
> "No, what did you want to do?"
>
> "Be a writer of course. I always wanted to be a writer."
>
> So there is no escape. Choice is an illusion, rebellion is a mad dash on a long leash. She smiled at me, a funny, wry smile. She'd showed her hand at last.
>
> And I'd thought I was his girl.[36]

In Ireland, Hampl finally comes to understand the real dynamic of her own childhood. Of her return, she says, "We flew home from Shannon. Nothing bad had happened—I couldn't believe it. Better than that. Ireland had been a revelation. *She* had been a revelation, I realized, dumfounded."[37]

33. Patricia Hampl, *The Florist's Daughter* (Orlando: Harcourt, 2007).

34. Hampl, *A Romantic Education* (New York: W.W. Norton, 1999).

35. Hampl, *The Florist's Daughter*, 136.

36. Ibid., 200–201.   37. Ibid., 140.

Secular Pilgrimages

A pattern emerges: "She'd shown her hand at last" (Hampl); "Ma made more sense to me now" (MacDonald); "the lessons of my own place" (Cusick); all sincere variations on what the MasterCard commercial suggests could be the worthwhile outcome of incurring credit card debt: "Finally understanding where your mother's coming from."

These memoirs suggest that the parents' truest self is the one found in Ireland. Away from the familiar and newly in touch with the forgotten or repressed Irish dimension in one's family history, it becomes possible to appreciate and connect with the parent in a more meaningful way. Sheehan's *Chasing the Hawk* makes that point explicit. While watching his long-remote and previously estranged father reconnect with his family and reconcile himself with his own impending death in Sligo, Donegal, and Belfast, Sheehan comes to the conclusion that "perhaps he was not so much a new man as the man he had always been. It was as if the real person, who had always been hidden—the one who was too wrapped up in anger and fear—had finally made his way to the surface."[38]

The question remains whether this is a matter of the child perceiving the "truest" self, or of the parent finally feeling comfortable enough, safe enough to reveal that self. Perhaps it cannot be answered; though if we assume that the imagined "Irish Pastoral" has shaped the travelers' expectations, then the latter explanation would be more likely: that life in real-time America has demanded that we put on masks, play artificial parts: a variation on the classic dichotomy between the corrupt city and the virtuous pastoral, with post-immigration America being the façade and Ireland the place where authenticity is possible.

The sense that an old wall around the parent has been lowered appears in all of these nonfiction works. Peter Quinn's essay "Stones of Memory" in *Looking for Jimmy* closes with a moment in which mother and son realize that no paper trail survives to link her to her immigrant forebears:

38. Sheehan, *Chasing the Hawk*, 256.

There wasn't even a faded scrawl on a mouldering baptismal registry to connect us to these empty, mist-shrouded fields.

My mother and I left the others on the church steps and walked together down an unpaved road. Nearby was a crumbling concrete barn with a rusted iron roof. There was a radio on. I looked at my mother. I knew she was still deeply grieved by my father's death, and I was afraid the utter absence of any trace of her own father, of a past gone and forever beyond reach, might bring her to tears.

The mist was once more changing to rain. "We should go back," I said.

"Listen," She said. I heard the quick fluctuations of fiddles coming from the radio, Irish sounds. "My father sang that tune."

She smiled and lifted her coat above her thin ankles and did a small graceful jig, the soles of her American shoes gently slapping the ground. It was a step I'd never seen her do before.[39]

In exactly that moment of connection, seemingly deeper than the disconnection of the vanished written record, Quinn is afforded a glimpse of his mother revealing a new and unsuspected affinity to her own past.

In MacDonald's memoir, he realizes while at the home of a relative in Ireland that his mother has been covering up her physical pain and personal turmoil for years: "Ma looked like a different person in this room. She was holding her back, and I noticed that she walked like she was a little sore. Like an older person with arthritis. Her face had changed too, and her voice was deeper, not the high note she was always hitting for everyone else."[40]

In Tobin's trip to Ireland, though his mother's response disappoints him, the journey effects something transformative in his relationship to his father. He begins to realize that his father, too, has an interior life and feels the weight of his forebears' pains. The short poem "Near Nag's Head" explores the discovery. Watching his father stand at a headland, the poet reflects that

39. Peter Quinn, "Stones of Memory," in *Looking for Jimmy: A Search for Irish America* (New York: Overlook Press, 2007), 83–84.

40. MacDonald, *Easter Rising*, 240–41.

Secular Pilgrimages

> He could be his own father's grandfather
> the way he stands before the rail
> as others stood before the hold, the blind
> journey before them, and nods to me
> in recognition despite the ocean between us.
>
> Even he knows on these cliffs the dead
> are reading aloud from the book of the wind.[41]

It is a more tangible book in "Tourmekeady Snow" that brings a moment of epiphany, when Cusick's father and his brother read a parish register that, to their appalled recognition, at last discloses the unspoken story of the family:

> My father held the book in his lap, the weight of each page falling upon his hand, and then stopped with a start when he found the entry for his father's family. He was silent for a few moments, then handed the book to John whose characteristic stern stare broke. "Jesus Christ," John said softly, "the old man left them all—three sisters and two brothers."
>
> I watched an invisible weight lessen upon my father as he learned this, a breath released from his lungs upon finally knowing something.[42]

We see this sense of letting go in Murphy's memoir as well, where he specifically speaks of the sense of release that he sees in his father:

> And then a moment that closes all distances.
> One of the men looks up and says, "Is it Packy Murphy?" There he is, Patrick Joseph Murphy, looking all too American in his Sears and Roebuck best, but he is surely close to home.
> "Packy?"
> No hesitation. "John Francis?"
> Obviously, Daddy had recognized John Francis Mulvey or, at least suspected that he did. No dramatic hugs—a quiet handshake, and

---

41. Tobin, "Near Nag's Head," in *Narrows*, 129.
42. Cusick, "Tourmakeady Snow," 56.

Mulvey, "We knew you were coming home. Eddie's expecting you above."[43]

Murphy says of the moment, "I remember it as a great release for Daddy." He later adds, "Great distances were closed in that meeting of two brothers who hadn't seen each other in forty years."[44]

However moving this moment of bridging the gap between brothers may be, it is the newly formed link between parent and child that animates these memoirs. Often, the parent's story and the child's story begin to seep into one another: in the act of watching the parent coming to terms with an old wound, the child is also healed. Murphy says that he had known Ireland "instinctively," and the memoir closes, "All along on that trip, I thought I was taking my Dad home. Now, I know he was showing me my own starting place. He took me home."[45]

And so we come back again to the mother and daughter in the commercial; the end point of their journey is shown in the print version of the advertisement that appeared in American magazines. The image selected is a moment in a pub, with the two women leaning close to one another, suggesting an ease with one another that we do not need to be told they have never experienced before. There are some subtle changes in the text: although the scene is unmistakably Irish, the name of the country goes unmentioned in the print version. Second, and more important, the reward, the phrase that states what is most valuable, is slightly different. In the print version, it is now in the past tense, "where your mother *was* coming from." That simple change of word effects a significant reassignment of what is revealed: understanding not your mother in Ireland, but your mother who behaved in such a baffling, inscrutable way when you were a child.

Whether or not aware of his or her own woundedness at the beginning of the trip with the parent, in all of these stories Ireland

43. Murphy, "Finding Home," 46–47.
44. Ibid., 47.
45. Ibid., 48.

Secular Pilgrimages

has been the site for a gift of healing—a family-based analog to the believers' faith in pilgrimage, or, in a counseling setting, to an individual patient's faith in a wise man or woman who knows us better than we know ourselves.

And what else can be said of such a gift, except to say that it is, well, priceless?

Bibliography

Allen, Steve. *The Funny Men*. New York: Simon and Schuster, 1956.

Almeida, Linda Dowling. *Irish Immigrants in New York City, 1945–1995*. Bloomington, Ind.: University of Indiana Press, 2001.

Appel, Martin. *Slide, Kelly, Slide: The Wild Life and Times of Mike "King" Kelly*. Lanham, Md.: Scarecrow Press, 1996.

Arthur, Chris. *Irish Nocturnes*. Aurora, Colo.: Davies Group, 1999.

"Barbara Mullen, 64, An Actress; First Appeared on the Stage at 3." *New York Times*, March 10, 1979.

"Barbara Mullen." Obituary. *Daily Telegraph*, March 10, 1979.

Barrett, James R. *The Irish Way: Becoming American in the Multi-Ethnic City*. New York: Penguin, 2012.

Barry, Dan. *Pull Me Up: A Memoir*. New York: W. W. Norton, 2004.

Battaglia, Steven. "The Biz: The Research Memo that Almost Killed *Seinfeld. TV Guide*, June 27, 2014.

Bayor, Ronald. *Neighbors in Conflict: The Irish, Germans, Jews, and Italians of New York City, 1929–1941*. Chicago: University of Illinois Press, 1988.

Bayor, Ronald, and Timothy Meagher, eds. *The New York Irish*. Baltimore: Johns Hopkins University Press, 1996.

Beers, David. *Blue Sky Dream: A Memoir of America's Fall from Grace*. New York: Harcourt Brace, 1996.

Berrigan, Daniel. *To Dwell in Peace: An Autobiography*. San Francisco: Harper and Row, 1987.

Betts, John R. "John Boyle O'Reilly and the American Paideia." *Éire-Ireland* 2, no. 4 (Winter 1967): 36–52.

Beuka, Robert. *SuburbiaNation: Reading Suburban Landscapes in Twentieth-*

Bibliography

Century American Fiction and Film. New York: Palgrave MacMillan, 2004.

Bishop, Jim. *The Golden Ham: A Candid Biography of Jackie Gleason*. New York: Simon and Schuster, 1956.

Blessing, Patrick. "The Irish." In *The Harvard Encyclopedia of American Ethnic Groups*, edited by Stephen Thernstrom, 524–45. Cambridge, Mass.: Harvard University Press, 1980.

——. "Irish Emigration to the United States: An Overview." In *The Irish in America: Emigration, Assimilation, and Impact*, edited by P. J. Drudy. Irish Studies 4. Cambridge: Cambridge University Press, 1985.

Bly, Robert. *Iron John: A Book about Men*. Reading, Mass.: Addison-Wesley, 1990.

Boland, Eavan. *Object Lessons: The Life of the Woman and the Poet in Our Time*. New York: W. W. Norton, 1996.

——. "Famine Roads." In *Irish Hunger: Personal Reflections on the Legacy of the Famine*, edited by Tom Hayden, 221. Niwot, Colo.: Roberts Rinehart, 1997.

Brogan, Kathleen. *Cultural Haunting: Ghosts and Ethnicity in Recent American Literature*. Charlottesville: University Press of Virginia. 1998.

Brown, Thomas. *Irish-American Nationalism, 1870–1900*. Westport, Conn: Greenwood, 1980.

Buber, Martin. *I and Thou*. New York: Charles Scribner and Sons, 1937.

Byrne, Lauren. "A Southie Homecoming: Michael Patrick MacDonald Talks to Lauren Byrne about Growing Up in South Boston." *Irish America Magazine*, February–March 2007.

Byron, Reginald. *Irish America*. New York: Oxford University Press, 1999.

Carson, Ciaran. *Last Night's Fun: A Book about Traditional Irish Music*. New York: Macmillan, 1996.

Casway, Jerrold. *Ed Delahanty in the Emerald Age of Baseball*. Notre Dame: University of Notre Dame Press, 2004.

Clark, Dennis. *Hibernia America: The Irish and Regional Cultures*. Westport, Conn: Greenwood, 1986.

Coady, Michael. "The Letter." In *Oven Lane*, 26–30. Oldcastle: Gallery, 1987.

———. *All Souls*. Oldcastle, County Meath: Gallery, 1997.

Cochrane, Feargal. *The End of Irish America? Globalisation and the Irish Diaspora*. Dublin: Irish Academic Press, 2010.

Cody, David. "The Gentleman." *The Victorian Web*. http://www.victorianweb.org/history/gentleman.html.

Coleman, Marie. *The Irish Sweep: A History of the Irish Hospitals Sweepstake, 1930–87*. Dublin: University College Dublin Press, 2009.

Connolly, James J. *The Triumph of Ethnic Progressivism: Urban Political Culture in Boston, 1900–1925*. Cambridge, Mass.: Harvard University Press, 1998.

Corbett, James J. *The Roar of the Crowd: The Rise and Fall of a Champion*. New York: G. P. Putnam's Sons, 1925.

Cosgrove, Olivia, Laurence Cox, Carmen Kuhling, and Peter Mulholland, eds. *Ireland's New Religious Movements*. Newcastle: Cambridge Scholars Press, 2011.

Countryman, John, and Kelly Matthews, eds. *The Country of the Young: Interpretations of Youth and Childhood in Irish Culture*. Dublin: Four Courts, 2013.

Covington, Dennis. *Salvation on Sand Mountain: Snake-Handling and Redemption in Southern Appalachia*. Reading, Mass: Addison-Wesley, 1995.

Crescenti, Peter, and Bob Columbe. *The Official Honeymooners Treasury*. New York: Galahad, 1989.

Darrach, Brad. "A Fond Goodbye to the Great One." *People* 28, no 2, July 13, 1987.

Davis, Ted. *Connie Mack: A Life in Baseball*. Bloomington, Ind.: iUniverse, 2000.

Diner, Hasia R. *Erin's Daughters in America: Irish Immigrant Women in the Nineteenth Century*. Baltimore: Johns Hopkins University Press, 1983.

Dougherty, Jane Elizabeth. "Nuala O'Faolain and the Unwritten Irish Girlhood." *New Hibernia Review* 11, no 2 (Summer 2007): 50–65.

Dowd, Christopher. *The Construction of Irish Identity in American Literature*. New York: Routledge, 2011.

Drudy, P. J. *The Irish in America: Emigration, Assimilation, and Impact*. Irish Studies 4. Cambridge: Cambridge University Press, 1985.

Bibliography

Duffy, Charles F. *A Family of His Own: A Life of Edwin O'Connor.* Washington, D.C.: The Catholic University of America Press, 2003.

Dunne, Finley Peter. *Mr. Dooley and the Chicago Irish: The Autobiography of a Nineteenth-Century Ethnic Group.* Edited by Charles Fanning. Washington, D.C.: The Catholic University of America Press, 1987.

Dunne, Joseph, and James Kelly, eds. *Childhood and Its Discontents: The First Seamus Heaney Lectures.* Dublin: Liffey, 2003.

Ebest, Ron. *Private Histories: The Writing of Irish Americans, 1900–1935.* Notre Dame: University of Notre Dame Press, 2005.

Ebest, Sally Barr. *The Banshees: A Literary History of Irish American Women Writers.* Syracuse: Syracuse University Press, 2013.

Ebest, Sally Barr, and Kathleen McInerney, eds. *Too Smart to Be Sentimental: Contemporary Irish American Women Writers.* Notre Dame: University of Notre Dame Press, 2008.

"Eleven Tales to Inspire Your First Trip to Ireland." http://www.infiniteireland.com/tales-to-inspire-your-first-trip-to-ireland/.

Erie, Stephen. *Rainbow's End: Irish-Americans and the Dilemmas of Urban Machine Politics, 1840–1985.* Berkeley: University of California Press, 1990.

Evans, A. G. *Fanatic Heart: A Life of John Boyle O'Reilly, 1844–1890.* Nedlands: University of Western Australia Press, 1999.

Fallows, Marjorie. *Irish Americans: Identity and Assimilation.* Englewood Cliffs, N.J.: Prentice Hall, 1979.

Fanning, Charles F. *The Exiles of Erin: Nineteenth-Century Irish-American Fiction.* Notre Dame: University of Notre Dame Press, 1987.

——. *The Irish Voice in America: 250 Years of Irish American Fiction.* Lexington: University Press of Kentucky, 1990.

——. ed. *New Perspectives on the Irish Diaspora.* Carbondale: Southern Illinois University Press, 2000.

——. *Mapping Norwood: An Irish American Memoir.* Amherst and Boston: University of Massachusetts Press, 2010.

——. "George McManus and Irish America." *ImageTexT: Interdisciplinary Comics Studies* 7, no 2 (2013).

Farrell, James T. *Young Lonigan.* New York: Vanguard, 1932.

——. *The Young Manhood of Studs Lonigan.* New York: Vanguard, 1934.

———. *Judgment Day*. New York: Vanguard, 1935.

Fisher, James T. "Alternative Sources of Catholic Intellectual Vitality." *U.S. Catholic Historian* 13, no. 1 (1995): 81–94.

———. *On the Irish Waterfront: The Crusader, the Movie, and the Soul of the Port of New York*. Ithaca: Cornell University Press, 2009.

Flanagan, Thomas. *The Year of the French*. New York: Holt, Rinehart, Winston, 1979.

———. *There You Are: Writings on Irish and American Literature and History*. Edited by Christopher Cahill. New York: New York Review of Books, 2004.

"The Flintstones: Trivia." http://www.imdb.com/title/tt0053502/trivia.

Forbes, Shannon. "Performative Identity Formation in Frank McCourt's *Angela's Ashes: A Memoir*." *Journal of Narrative Theory* 37, no. 3 (2007): 473–96.

Foster, Roy. "'Tisn't: The Million-Dollar Blarney of the McCourts." *New Republic*, November 1, 1999.

Foucault, Michel. *Discipline and Punish: The Birth of the Prison*. Translated by Alan Sheridan. New York: Vintage, 1999.

Funchion, Michael, ed. *Irish Voluntary Organizations*. Westport, Conn.: Greenwood, 1983.

Gallop, Jane. *Reading Lacan*. Ithaca: Cornell University Press, 1985.

Galvin, Brendan. *Raising Irish Walls*. Bristol, R.I.: Ampersand, 1989.

———. *Saints in Their Ox-Hide Boat*. Baton Rouge: Louisiana State University Press, 1991.

Gans, Herbert J. "Symbolic Ethnicity: The Future of Ethnic Groups and Cultures in America." *Ethnic and Racial Studies* 2, no. 1 (1979): 1–20.

Gillespie, Michael Patrick. *The Myth of an Irish Cinema: Approaching Irish-Themed Films*. Syracuse: Syracuse University Press, 2008.

Glazier, Michael, ed. *The Encyclopedia of the Irish in America*. Notre Dame: University of Notre Dame Press, 1999.

Greaney, Áine. "Is Ireland Really 'Home?' Used to Be? Wanna Be? Never Be?," http://www.irishabroad.com/Blogs/Posts.aspx?date=2013-09&bid=31398.

Greeley, Andrew M. *The Church and the Suburbs*. New York: Sheed and Ward, 1959.

Bibliography

——. *That Most Distressful Nation: The Taming of the American Irish.* Chicago: Quadrangle, 1972.

——. *The Irish Americans: The Rise to Money and Power.* New York: Warner, 1993.

Hagan, Edward A. "Really An Alley Cat?: *Angela's Ashes* and Critical Orthodoxy." *New Hibernia Review* 4, no. 4 (2000): 39–52.

——. *Goodbye Yeats and O'Neill: Farce in Contemporary Irish and Irish-American Narratives.* Amsterdam: Rodopi, 2010.

Haley, Alex. *Roots: The Saga of an American Family.* New York: Doubleday, 1976.

Hampl, Patricia. *A Romantic Education.* New York: W. W. Norton, 1999.

——. *The Florist's Daughter.* Orlando: Harcourt, 2007.

Harburg, E. Y., and Fred Saidy. *Finian's Rainbow.* Music and lyrics by Burton Lane and Yip Harburg. New York: Random House, 1947.

Harte, Liam, ed. *Modern Irish Autobiography: Self, Nation and Society.* Houndsmills and New York: Palgrave MacMillan, 2007.

——. *A History of Irish Autobiography.* 2 vols. Cambridge: Cambridge University Press, 2017.

Hayden, Tom, ed. *Irish Hunger: Personal Reflections on the Legacy of the Famine.* Niwot, Colo.: Roberts Rinehart, 1997.

——. *Irish on the Inside: In Search of the Soul of Irish America.* New York: Verso, 2001.

Hayne, Donald. *Batter My Heart.* New York: Knopf, 1963.

Heaney, Seamus. *Station Island.* London: Faber and Faber, 1984.

Hendrix, Harville. *Getting the Love You Want: A Guide for Couples.* New York: Macmillan, 2001.

Henry, William A., II. *The Great One: The Life and Legend of Jackie Gleason.* New York: Doubleday, 1992.

Holmquist, Kate. "Falling in Love with Ireland." *Irish Times,* magazine section, September 2, 2006.

Ibson, John Duffy. *Will the World Break Your Heart? Dimensions and Consequences of Irish American Assimilation.* New York: Garland, 1990.

"Inflation Calculator." http://data.bls.gov/cgi-bin/cpicalc.pl.

Isenberg, Michael T. *John L. Sullivan and His America.* Urbana: University of Illinois Press, 1988.

Jacobson, Matthew Frye. *Special Sorrows: The Diasporic Imagination of Irish, Polish, and Jewish Immigrants in the United States.* Cambridge, Mass.: Harvard University Press, 1995.

———. *Roots Too: White Ethnic Revival in Post–Civil Rights America.* Cambridge, Mass.: Harvard University Press, 2009.

Jeffares, A. Norman. *A New Commentary on the Poems of W. B. Yeats.* Stanford: Stanford University Press, 1984.

Joyce, James. *Ulysses.* Edited by Hans Walter Gabler. New York: Random House, 1986.

Kazal, Russell. "Revisiting Assimilation: The Rise, Fall and Reappraisal of a Concept in American Ethnic History." *American Historical Review* 100, no. 2 (1995): 437–71.

Kavanaugh, James A. *A Modern Priest Looks at His Outdated Church.* New York: Trident, 1967.

Kelleher, John V. *Selected Writings of John V. Kelleher on Ireland and Irish America.* Edited by Charles F. Fanning. Carbondale: Southern Illinois University Press, 2002.

Keller, James. *To Light a Candle: The Autobiography of James Keller, Founder of the Christophers.* Garden City, N.Y.: Doubleday, 1963.

Kelley, Francis Clement. *The Bishop Jots It Down: An Autobiographical Strain on Words.* New York: Harper, 1948. Originally published in 1939.

Kelly, Mary C. *Ireland's Great Famine in Irish-American History: Enshrining a Fateful Memory.* Lanham, Md.: Rowman and Littlefield, 2014.

Kennedy, John F. "Remarks at Eyre Square, Galway, June 29, 1963." *Public Papers of the Presidents of the United States: John F. Kennedy, 1963.* Washington, D.C.: Government Printing Office, 1964.

Kennedy, William. *Ironweed.* New York: Viking, 1983.

Kenny, Kevin. *Making Sense of the Molly Maguires.* New York: Oxford University Press, 1998.

———. *The American Irish: A History.* New York: Longman, 2000.

———, ed. *New Directions in Irish-American History.* Madison: University of Wisconsin Press, 2003.

Kermode, Frank. *The Sense of an Ending: Studies in the Theory of Fiction.* New York: Oxford University Press, 1967.

Bibliography

Kuklick, Bruce. *To Every Thing a Season: Shibe Park and Urban Philadelphia, 1909–1976*. Princeton: Princeton University Press, 1993.

Kunkel, Thomas. *Man in Profile: Joseph Mitchell of "The New Yorker."* New York: Random House, 2015.

Land, Bernhard, and Colleen McDannell. *Heaven: A History*. New Haven: Yale University Press, 1988.

Lee, J. J., and Marion R. Casey, eds. *Making the Irish American: History and Heritage of the Irish in the United States*. New York: New York University Press, 2006.

Lehr, Dick, and Gerard O'Neill. *Black Mass: The True Story of an Unholy Alliance between the FBI and the Irish Mob*. New York: HarperCollins Perennial, 2000.

Leigh, David. *Circuitous Journeys: Modern Spiritual Autobiography*. New York: Fordham University Press, 2000.

Lerner, Laurence. *Angels and Absences: Child Deaths in the Nineteenth Century*. Nashville: Vanderbilt University Press, 1997.

Liddy, James. *On American Literature and Diasporas*. Edited by Eamonn Wall. Galway: Arlen House, 2013.

Lipsitz, George. *Time Passages: Collective Memory and American Popular Culture*. Minneapolis: University of Minnesota Press, 1990.

Luddy, Maria, and James Smith, eds. *Children, Childhood and Irish Society, 1500 to the Present*. Dublin: Four Courts, 2014.

Lynch, Claire. *Irish Autobiography: Stories of Self in the Narrative of a Nation*. Bern: Peter Lang, 2009.

MacDonald, Michael Patrick. *All Souls: A Family Story from Southie*. New York: Ballantine, 1999.

——. *Easter Rising: An Irish American Coming Up from Under*. Boston: Houghton Mifflin, 2006.

MacGowan, Michael. *The Hard Road to Klondike*. Translated by Valentin Iremonger. London: Routledge and Kegan Paul, 1973.

Macht, Norman L. *Connie Mack and the Early Years of Baseball*. Lincoln: University of Nebraska Press, 2007.

Mack, Connie. *Connie Mack's Baseball Book*. New York: Alfred A. Knopf, 1950.

——. *My Sixty-Six Years in the Big Leagues*. Mineola, N.Y.: Dover, 2009.

Marks, Edward B. *They All Sang: From Tony Pastor to Rudy Vallee*. As told to A. J. Liebling. New York: Viking Press, 1935.

Martinson, Tom. *American Dreamscape: The Pursuit of Happiness in Postwar Suburbia*. New York: Carroll and Graf, 2000.

Mays, John Bentley. *Power in the Blood: Land, Memory, and a Southern Family*. New York: HarperCollins, 1996.

McCaffrey, Lawrence J. *The Irish Diaspora in America*. Bloomington: Indiana University Press, 1976.

———. *Textures of Irish America*. Syracuse: Syracuse University Press, 1992.

McClinton-Temple, Jennifer. "Expressing 'Irishness' in Three Irish-American Autobiographies." *New Hibernia Review* 17, no. 2 (2013): 103–18.

McCourt, Frank. *Angela's Ashes: A Memoir*. New York: Scribner's, 1996.

———. *'Tis: A Memoir*. New York: Scribner's, 1999.

———. *Teacher Man*. New York: Scribner's, 2005.

McDannell, Colleen. *Material Christianity: Religion and Popular Culture in America*. New Haven: Yale University Press, 1995.

McGinley, Gerard. *A Trappist Writes Home: Letters of Abbot Gerard McGinley, OCSO, to his Family*. Milwaukee: Bruce, 1960.

McGreevy, John T. "Thinking on One's Own: Catholicism in the American Intellectual Imagination, 1928–1960." *Journal of American History* 84, no. 1 (1997): 97–131.

McNulty, John. *Third Avenue, New York*. Boston: Little, Brown, 1946.

———. "Back Where I Had Never Been." *New Yorker*, September 10, 1949.

———. *A Man Gets Around*. Boston: Little Brown, 1951.

———. *The World of John McNulty*. New York: Doubleday, 1957.

Meadows, Audrey. *Love, Alice: My Life as a Honeymooner*. New York: Crown, 1994.

Meagher, Timothy J., ed. *From Paddy to Studs: Irish-American Communities in the Turn of the Century Era, 1880–1920*. Westport, Conn.: Greenwood, 1986.

———. *Inventing Irish America: Generation, Class and Ethnicity in a New England City, 1880–1928*. Notre Dame: University of Notre Dame Press, 2001.

———. *The Columbia Guide to Irish American History*. New York: Columbia University Press, 2005.

Bibliography

Merton, Thomas. *The Seven Storey Mountain*. New York: Harcourt Brace, 1948.

Miller, Kerby. *Emigrants and Exiles: Ireland and the Irish Exodus to North America*. New York: Oxford University Press, 1985.

Mitchell, James B. "Popular Autobiography as Historiography: The Reality Effect of *Angela's Ashes*." *Biography* 26, no. 4 (2003): 607–24.

Mitchell, Joseph. *My Ears Are Bent*. New York: Sheridan House, 1938.

———. *Joe Gould's Secret*. New York: Viking, 1965.

———. *Up in the Old Hotel*. New York: Pantheon, 1992.

———. *The Bottom of the Harbor*. New York: Modern Library, 1994.

Montague, John. *The Dead Kingdom*. Oxford: Oxford University Press, 1984.

———. *Born in Brooklyn: John Montague's America*. Edited by David Lampe. Fredonia, N.Y.: White Pine Press, 1991.

Moore, George. "Home Sickness." In *The Untilled Field*, 21–31. Gerrards Cross: Colin Smythe, 2000.

Morgan, Jack. *New World Irish: Notes on One Hundred Years of Lives and Letters in American Culture*. New York: Palgrave Macmillan, 2011.

Moynihan, Daniel P. "The Irish." In *Beyond the Melting Pot: The Negroes, Puerto Ricans, Jews, Italians, and Irish of New York City*, edited by Daniel Moynihan and Nathan Glazer, 219–87. Cambridge, Mass.: Massachusetts Institute of Technology Press, 1970.

Mullen, Barbara. *Life Is My Adventure*. New York: Coward-McCann, 1937.

Mullen, Pat. *Man of Aran*. New York: E. P. Dutton, 1935.

———. *Hero Breed: A Novel*. New York: R. M. McBride, 1937.

———. *Come Another Day*. London: Faber and Faber, 1940.

Murphy, Edward F. *Yankee Priest: An Autobiographical Journey, with Certain Detours, from Salem to New Orleans*. Garden City, N.Y.: Doubleday, 1952.

Negra, Diane, ed. *The Irish in Us: Irishness, Performativity, and Popular Culture*. Durham: Duke University Press, 2006.

New Catholic Encyclopedia. New York: McGraw Hill, 1967.

Newman, John Henry. *Apologia Pro Vita Sua*. New York: Longmans, 1908.

O'Brien, George. "The Last Word: Reflections on *Angela's Ashes*." In *New Perspectives on the Irish Diaspora*, edited by Charles Fanning, 236–49. Carbondale, Ill.: Southern Illinois University Press, 2000.

O'Brien, Matthew J. "Irishness in Great Britain and the United States: Transatlantic and Cross-Channel Migration Networks and Irish Ethnicity, 1920–90." Ph.D. diss., University of Wisconsin, 2001.

O'Brien, Michael J. *A Hidden Phase of American History: Ireland's Part in America's Struggle for Liberty.* New York: Dodd, Mead, 1919.

O'Connell, Shaun. "That Much Credit: Irish-American Identity and Writing." *Massachusetts Review* 44, nos. 1–2 (2003): 251–68.

The Official Catholic Directory Anno Domini 1960. New York: P. J. Kenedy and Sons, 1960.

O'Hanlon, Ray. *The New Irish Americans.* Niwot, Colo.: Roberts Reinhart, 1998.

O'Reilly, John Boyle. *Ethics of Boxing and Manly Sport.* Boston: Ticknor and Sons, 1888.

O'Sullivan, Patrick, ed. *The Irish World Wide: History, Heritage, Identity.* Leicester, U.K.: Leicester University Press. Vol. 1, *Patterns of Migration,* 1992. Vol. 2, *The Irish in the New Communities,* 1992. Vol. 3, *The Creative Migrant,* 1994. Vol. 4, *Irish Women and Irish Migration,* 1995. Vol. 5, *Religion and Identity,* 1996.

Ozorak, Elizabeth Weiss. "The View from the Edge: Pilgrimage and Transformation." In *On the Road to Being There: Studies in Pilgrimage and Tourism in Late Modernity,* 61–82. Leiden: Koninklijke Brill NV, 2006.

Perrin, Noel. "Paragon of Reporters: Joseph Mitchell." *Sewanee Review* 91, no. 2 (Spring 1983): 167–84.

Pioreck, Ricard. "Baseball and Vaudeville in the Development of Popular Culture in the United States, 1880–1930." In *The Cooperstown Symposium on Baseball and American Culture, 1999,* 83–100. Jefferson, N.C.: McFarland, 2000.

Powell, John, SJ. *Why Am I Afraid to Tell You Who I Am?* Niles, Ill.: Argus Communications, 1969.

Powers, J. F. *Prince of Darkness and Other Stories.* Garden City, N.Y.: Doubleday, 1947.

——. *The Presence of Grace.* Garden City, N.Y.: Doubleday, 1956.

Quinn, Dermot. *The Irish in New Jersey: Four Centuries of American Life.* New Brunswick: Rutgers University Press, 2004.

Bibliography

Quinn, Peter. *Looking for Jimmy: A Search for Irish America*. New York: Overlook Press, 2007.

Rains, Stephanie. *The Irish-American in Popular Culture, 1945–2000*. Dublin: Irish Academic Press, 2007.

Raleigh, John Henry. "O'Neill's *Long Day's Journey Into Night* and New England Irish-Catholicism." In *O'Neill: A Collection of Critical Essays*, edited by John Gassner, 125–41. Englewood Cliffs, N.J.: Prentice-Hall, 1964.

Reisman, David. *The Lonely Crowd: A Study in the Changing American Character*. New Haven: Yale University Press, 1950.

Remnick, David. "Postscript: Joseph Mitchell; Three Generations of *New Yorker* Writers Remember the City's Incomparable Chronicler." *New Yorker*, June 10, 1996.

"Return to Murder." *Guardian*, July 30, 1975.

Rhea, Mimi. *I Was Jacqueline Kennedy's Dressmaker*. New York: Popular Library, 1963.

Richstater, Thomas. *Liturgical Law Today: New Style, New Spirit*. Chicago: Franciscan Herald Press, 1977.

Robinson, Henry Morton. *The Cardinal*. New York: Simon and Schuster, 1950.

Robinson, Tim. "Listening to the Landscape." In *Setting Foot on the Shores of Connemara and Other Writings*, 151–64. Dublin: Lilliput, 2007.

Rockett, Kevin. *The Irish Filmography*. Dublin: Red Mountain Press, 1996.

Roediger, David. *The Wages of Whiteness: Race and the Making of the American Working Class*. New York: Verso, 1991.

Rogers, James Silas, ed. *Extended Family: Essays on Being Irish American from "New Hibernia Review."* Chester Springs, Pa.: Dufour Editions, 2013.

Rogers, James Silas, and Matthew J. O'Brien, eds. *After the Flood: Irish America, 1945–1960*. Dublin: Irish Academic Press, 2009.

Schrier, Arnold. *Ireland and the Irish Emigration, 1850–1900*. Minneapolis: University of Minnesota Press, 1958.

Shannon, Christopher. *Bowery to Broadway: The American Irish in Classic Hollywood Cinema*. Scranton: University of Scranton Press, 2010.

Shannon, William V. *The American Irish: A Social and Political History*. New York: Macmillan, 1963.

Sheed, Wilfred. *Three Mobs: Labor, Church and Mafia*. New York: Sheed and Ward, 1974.

———. "Mr. Mack and the Main Chance." In *The Ultimate Baseball Book*, edited by Daniel Okrent and Harris Lewine, 105–20. Boston: Houghton Mifflin, 1979.

Sheehan, Andrew. *Chasing the Hawk: Looking for My Father, Finding Myself*. New York: Delacorte Press, 2002.

Sheen, Fulton. *Treasure in Clay: The Autobiography of Fulton J. Sheen*. Garden City, N.Y.: Image, 1982.

Simon, Ron. "Ralph Kramden and *The Honeymooners* Turn the Big 5 0 (Sort Of)." *Television Quarterly* 36, no. 1 (2005): 59–65.

Sims, Norman, and James Rogers. "Joseph Mitchell." In *American Literary Journalists, 1945–1995 Dictionary of Literary Biography*, edited by Arthur Kaul, 185:199–210. Detroit: Gale Research, 1997.

Sollors, Werner, ed. *The Invention of Ethnicity*. New York: Oxford University Press, 1989.

Starr, Michael Seth. *Art Carney: A Biography*. New York: Fromm, 1997.

Statistical Abstract of the United States. Washington, D.C.: Government Printing Office, 1955.

Steinfels, Margaret O'Brien. "I Knew Angela, Did Frank McCourt?" *Commonweal* 124, no. 7 (November 7, 1997): 7–8.

Sullivan, John L. *Life and Reminiscences of a 19th-Century Gladiator*. Boston: J. A. Hearn, 1892.

———. *I Can Lick Any Sonofabitch in the House*. Edited by Gilbert Odd. London: Proteus, 1979.

Swidler, Leonard, and Paul Mojzes. *The Study of Religion in an Age of Global Dialogue*. Philadelphia: Temple University Press, 2000.

Taves, Ann. *The Household of Faith: Roman Catholic Devotions in Mid-Nineteenth-Century America*. Notre Dame: University of Notre Dame Press, 1986.

Taylor, Lawrence. *Occasions of Faith: An Anthropology of Irish Catholics*. Philadelphia: University of Pennsylvania Press, 1995.

Tobin, Daniel. *The Narrows*. New York: Four Way, 2005.

Bibliography

——. *Awake in America: On Irish American Poetry*. Notre Dame: Notre Dame University Press, 2011.

Trillin, Calvin. *Killings*. New York: Ticknor and Fields, 1984.

Tully, Jim. *Beggars of Life*. New York: Albert and Charles Boni, 1924.

——. *Shanty Irish*. New York: Albert and Charles Boni, 1928.

Tully, John Day. *Ireland and Irish Americans, 1932–1945: The Search for Identity*. Dublin: Irish Academic Press, 2010.

Vallely, Fintan. "The Making of a Lifelong *Companion*." *New Hibernia Review* 4, no. 2 (2000): 141–53.

Wall, Eamonn. *From the Sin-é Café to the Black Hills: Notes on the New Irish*. Madison: University of Wisconsin Press, 1999.

Waters, Mary C. *Ethnic Options: Choosing Identities in America*. Berkeley: University of California Press, 1990.

Waters, Maureen. *Crossing Highbridge: A Memoir of Irish America*. Syracuse: Syracuse University Press, 2001.

Watson, Julia. "Ordering the Family: Genealogy as Autobiographical Pedigree." In *Getting a Life: Everyday Uses of Autobiography*, edited by Sidonie Smith and Julia Watson, 297–326. Minneapolis: University of Minnesota Press, 1996.

Weatherby, W. J. *Jackie Gleason: An Intimate Portrait of the Great One*. New York: Pharos, 1992.

Wexman, Virginia Wright. "Returning from the Moon: Jackie Gleason and the Carnivalesque." In *Critiquing the Sitcom: A Reader*, edited by Joanne Morreale, 56–68. Syracuse: Syracuse University Press, 2013.

White, Eva Roa. "Emigration as Emancipation: Portrayals of the Immigrant Irish Girl in Nineteenth-Century Fiction." *New Hibernia Review* 9, no. 1 (2005): 95–108.

White, Richard. *Remembering Ahanagran: Storytelling in a Family's Past*. New York: Hill and Wang, 1998.

Wilcox, Ralph C. "The Shamrock and the Eagle: Irish Americans and Sport in the Nineteenth Century." In *Ethnicity and Sport in North American History and Culture*, edited by George Eisen and David K. Wiggins, 55–74. Westport, Conn.: Greenwood, 1994.

Williams, William H. A. *'Twas Only an Irishman's Dream: The Image of Ire-*

land and the Irish in American Popular Song Lyrics, 1800–1920. Urbana: University of Illinois Press, 1996.

———. "Green Again: Irish-American Lace-Curtain Satire." *New Hibernia Review* 6, no. 2 (2002): 9–24.

Wilson, Sloan. *The Man in the Gray Flannel Suit.* New York: Simon and Schuster, 1955.

Winch, Terence. *Irish Musicians/American Friends.* Minneapolis: Coffee House Press, 1985.

Winsberg, Morton D. "The Suburbanization of the Irish in Boston, Chicago, and New York." *Éire-Ireland* 21, no. 3 (1986): 90–104.

Witoszek, Nina, and Patrick F. Sheeran. *Talking to the Dead: A Study of Irish Funerary Traditions.* Amsterdam: Rodopi, 1998.

Yeats, William Butler. *Selected Poems and Four Plays of William Butler Yeats.* Edited by M. L. Rosenthal. New York: Scribner's, 1996.

Zuelow, Eric. *Making Ireland Irish: Tourism and National Identity Since the Irish Civil War.* Syracuse: Syracuse University Press, 2009.

Filmography

Bishop Fulton J: Sheen: His Irish Wit and Wisdom, Vision Video, DVD (2006).

The Commitments, directed by Alan Parker (1991).

Darby O'Gill and the Little People, directed by Robert Stevenson (1959).

Eat the Peach, directed by Peter Ormrod (1986).

An Everlasting Piece, directed by Barry Levinson (2000).

The Gentle Gunman, directed by Basil Dearden (1952).

Gentleman Jim, directed by Raoul Walsh (1942).

Going My Way, directed by Leo McCarey (1944).

The Halo Effect, directed by Lance Daly (2004).

In America, directed by Jim Sheridan (2002).

Intermission, directed by John Crowley (2003).

It Takes a Thief, directed by John Gilling (1960).

Jeannie, directed by Harold French (1941).

Man of Aran, directed by Robert Flaherty (1934).

MasterCard commercial, mother and daughter in Ireland, directed by Jim Sheridan (2001).

McSorley's New York, directed by Marcia Rock (1987).

Bibliography

My Left Foot, directed by Jim Sheridan (1999).

On the Waterfront, directed by Elia Kazan (1954).

Quackser Fortune Has a Cousin in the Bronx, directed by Waris Hussein (1970).

The Quiet Man, directed by John Ford (1952).

Spin the Bottle, directed by Ian Fitzgibbon (2004).

The Van, directed by Stephen Frears (1996).

The Very Edge, directed by Cyril Frankel (1963).

Waking Ned Devine, directed by Kirk Jones (1998).

When Brendan Met Trudy, directed by Kieron J. Walsh (2000).

You Can't Beat the Irish, directed by John Paddy Carstairs (1952).

Index

Index

Index

Irish-American Autobiography: The Divided Hearts of Athletes, Priests, Pilgrims, and More
was designed in Mrs Eaves XL Serif Nar with Quadraat Sans display and com-
posed by Kachergis Book Design of Pittsboro, North Carolina. It was printed on
60-pound Offset and bound by Thomson Reuters of Eagan, Minnesota.